Treatise on Prayer and Fasting

Āyatullāh Sayyid ʿAlī Khāminaʾī

AL-BURĀQ

Copyright

ISBN: 978-1-956276-62-6
Printed and published by al-Burāq Publications.
Translated and annotated by al-Burāq Publications. Where needed, context and transliterations were added. Some minor edits were made to the translated text.

www.al-Buraq.org
publications@al-Buraq.org

First Edition | February 2025

Dedication

The publication of this book was made possible through the generous support of our donors.

Please recite *Sūrat al-Fātihah* and ask God for the Divine reward (*thawāb*) to be conferred upon the donors and also the souls of all the deceased in whose memory their loved ones have contributed graciously towards the publication of *Treatise on Prayer and Fasting: A Bilingual Edition.*

We begin by giving all praise and thanks to God ﷻ for giving us the *tawfīq* to translate this book. He has guided us and without Him, we would not have been guided to the straight path embodied by the Prophet Muḥammad ﷺ and the Ahl al-Bayt عليهم السلام.

This book is dedicated to all the scholars, martyrs and believers who worked tirelessly to promote the pure Muḥammadan path.

We want to also give our thanks and appreciation to all believers from around the world and acknowledge the team which helped al-Burāq Publications complete this work, spending countless hours to make its publication possible. Please recite Sūrat al-Fātiḥah on behalf of them, their families, and their marḥūmīn.

This book is dedicated in honor of the following individuals. Please remember them in your prayers and may God ﷻ have mercy on them and their loved ones.

Abdul-Wahab Rustam
Abid Yawar
Ahmad S. Salame
Ali Beydoun
Ali Bin Hamid
Ali H. Hammoud
Ali Mansoor Zaidi
Alya Agemy
Azhar Ali
Azra Bokhari
Bande Khuda
Bilquis Fatimah
Elabed Aoun
Habib Makki
Habiba Sakha
Ḥajj Ali Hammoud
Ḥajj Haidar Alaouie
Ḥajj Ibrahim Abou Saleh
Ḥajj Youssef Ali Dabaja
Ḥajji Imane Srour
Mariam Ajami
Masood Akbar
Mirza Mohammed
Mirza Murtuza
Muhammad Rafiq
Munawwar Jehan
Rayhana Hammoud
Riaz Haider
Sabiha Jafri
Sahib al-Zaman
Sajad Gowhar
Salman Jafri
Saniyeh Bazzi
Sayed Khaled Abdallah
Sayed Khaled Saleh
Sayed Mahmoud Saleh
Sayyid Asad Jafri
Seknah Yassin
Shaandar Fatima
Shahab Raza

Ḥajji Intissar Bazzi
Hamida Bokhari
Hasan Zaheer
Intisar Ul Hasan
Jafer Haider
Leila Mansour
Mahmoud Tiba
Majeedah Begum
Majid Salemeh
Mallak Jaber
Sokna Makki
Syed M. Taqi
Syed Mehdi Rizvi
Syed Nawab Kazmi
Syed Nurul Jafri
Zahra Abbas
Zahraa Hammoud
Zainul Abedin Abbas
Zakia Mehdi

Duʿāʾ al-Ḥujjah

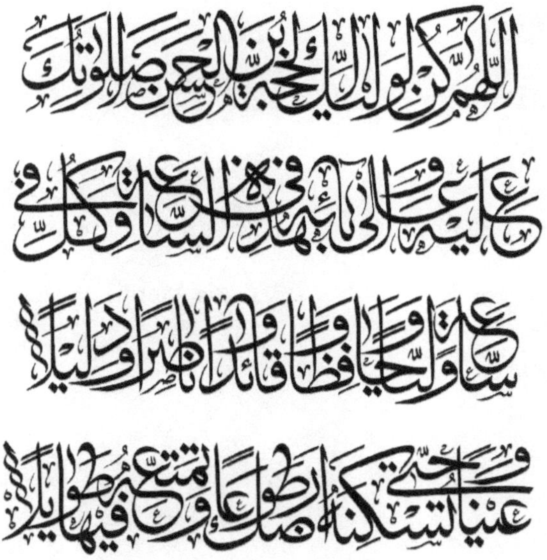

O God, be, for Your representative, the Ḥujjat (proof), son of al-Ḥasan, Your blessings be upon him and his forefathers, in this hour and in every hour: a guardian, a protector, a leader, a helper, a proof, and an eye—until You make him live on the Earth, in obedience (to You), and cause him to live in it for a long time.

Terms of Respect

The following Arabic phrases have been used throughout this book in their respective places to show the reverence which the noble personalities deserve.

عزّ وجلّ

Used for God, meaning:
Exalted and Sublime (Perfect) is He

صلى الله عليه وآله

Used for Prophet Muḥammad, meaning:
Blessings from God be upon him and his family

عليه السلام

Used for a man (singular) of a high status, meaning:
Peace be upon him

عليها السلام

Used for a woman (singular) of a high status, meaning:
Peace be upon her

عليهما السلام

Used for men/women (dual) of a high status, meaning:
Peace be upon them both

عليهم السلام

Used for men and/or women (plural) of a high status, meaning:
Peace be upon them all

عجّل الله تعالى فرجه الشريف

Used for Imām Muḥammad al-Mahdī, meaning:
May God hasten his return

قدس سره

Used for a deceased scholar, meaning:
May his resting [burial] place remain pure

Transliteration Table

The method of transliteration of Islāmic terminology from the Arabic language has been carried out according to the standard transliteration table below.

ء	ʾ	ر	r	ف	f
ا	a	ز	z	ق	q
ب	b	س	s	ك	k
ت	t	ش	sh	ل	l
ث	th	ص	ṣ	م	m
ج	j	ض	ḍ	ن	n
ح	ḥ	ط	ṭ	و	w
خ	kh	ظ	ẓ	ه	h
د	d	ع	ʿ	ي	y
ذ	dh	غ	gh		
Long Vowels					
ا	ā	و	ū	ي	ī
Short Vowels					
ـَـ	a	ـُـ	u	ـِـ	i

Table of Contents

aṣ-Ṣawm | Fasting 219

Iʿtikāf 271

Preface

بسم الله الرحمن الرحيم

In the Name of God, the Beneficent, the Merciful

The treatise in your hands corresponds to the latest fatwas of His Eminence, Āyatullāh Sayyid 'Alī Khāmina'ī, regarding matters related to the subjects of prayer, fasting, and i'tikāf.

"If we adhere to Islāmic rulings and if the Islāmic community follows the Islāmic faith combined with adherence to divine ordinances and laws, then the goal that humanity has sought throughout history is achieved. What does this mean? It means realizing comfort and material prosperity, drawing closer to perfection, developing and growing, and ascending spiritually. Ultimately, man aspires to be pure and enlightened... He derives spiritual pleasure from enlightenment, purity, and the worship of God."[1]

---

1 This excerpt is from a speech by His Eminence, in front of a large crowd of residents of Mashhad and visitors of Imām 'Alī ar-Riḍā's shrine, dated 5 Ramaḍān 1411, corresponding to the 21st day of March 1991.

aṣ-Ṣalāt | Prayer

Prayer [Ṣalāt] is the most important act of worship. Performing prayer correctly and with the presence of heart —putting one's heart fully—purifies man's heart and enlightens his soul, enabling him to distance himself from abominable and reprehensible morals. Ultimately, prayer can gradually purify the individual and society from all forms of impurity.

Essentially, prayer must be offered as soon as its time arrives, with a presence of heart and away from any sense of ostentation and showing off. During his prayer, the worshiper must recall that every word he utters is speaking to God ﷻ and thus be mindful of what he says.

The Obligatory Prayers

Issue 1: The obligatory prayers consist of the following:

1. Daily prayers.

2. The Prayer of Ṭawāf [Ṣalāt aṭ-Ṭawāf], which is performed after the obligatory [ritual] Ṭawāf [circumambulating] around the Kaʿbah.

3. The Prayer of the Signs [Ṣalāt al-Āyāt], which becomes obligatory during eclipses, lunar eclipses, earthquakes, and the like.

4. The Funeral Prayer [Ṣalāt al-Janāzah or Ṣalāt al-Mayyit], which is obligatory to be performed upon the body of the deceased Muslim.

5. Making up the missed obligatory prayers of the father by his eldest male child and making them up for his mother is a matter of obligatory precaution.

6. The prayer that becomes obligatory[2] due to a covenant, vow, oath, or contract.

Daily Obligatory Prayers

Issue 2: The daily prayers are among the most important acts of worship in Islāmic law; rather, they are the pillar of faith, and it is not permissible to abandon them under any circumstance.

Issue 3: The obligatory prayers constitute in total seventeen units of prayer [rakʿat], and they are the following:

1. Fajr [dawn] prayer (two units)

2. Ẓuhr [noon] prayer (four units)

3. ʿAṣr [afternoon] prayer (four units)

4. Maghrib [sunset] prayer (three units)

5. ʿIshāʾ [evening] prayer (four units)

---

[2] In reality, what is obligatory [in regards to prayer] is fulfilling a covenant, vow, oath, and contract. It does not mean that recommended or commendable [mustaḥabb] prayers turn into obligatory prayers.

Timing of Fajr Prayer

Issue 4: The time for Fajr prayer starts from the moment of dawn (true dawn)[3] and extends until sunrise.

Issue 5: There is no difference between moonlit and non-moonlit nights regarding the determination of the moment of dawn (the beginning time of the Fajr prayer). However, the worshiper should wait on moonlit nights until the whiteness of dawn overpowers the moonlight, then perform the prayer.

Timing of Ẓuhr and ʿAṣr Prayers

Issue 6: The time for Ẓuhr [noon] prayer begins from the onset of midday (decline of the sun after reaching its

---

[3] True dawn versus false dawn: False dawn is light that appears in the sky before true dawn. Instead of spreading horizontally across the horizon, it shines vertically upwards. True dawn is when soft white sunlight touching the horizon's surface appears and spreads across the horizon. Therefore, observing true dawn requires viewing from an open, dark, east-facing horizon. And that is why seeing it from inside cities is very difficult. Hence, since identifying true dawn accurately is difficult, it is prudent to delay prayer ten minutes after media channels broadcast the call to prayer [ādhān] as a precaution.

zenith, that is, Zawāl of the sun)[4] until only enough time remains to perform the obligatory ʿAṣr prayer before sunset.

Issue 7: The time for ʿAṣr [afternoon] prayer starts after the passing of the amount of time required to perform the Ẓuhr prayer from the onset of midday (Zawāl of the sun) until sunset.

Issue 8: Each of the Ẓuhr and ʿAṣr prayers has a specific time and a shared time. The specific time for Ẓuhr prayer is the period required to pray it from the onset of midday, and the specific time for ʿAṣr prayer is the period required to pray it before sunset. The remaining time between the specific times for Ẓuhr and ʿAṣr is shared between Ẓuhr and ʿAṣr prayers.

Issue 9: If the specific time for ʿAṣr prayer begins and the person has not yet prayed Ẓuhr, the Ẓuhr prayer becomes a missed or make-up prayer [qaḍāʾ], and it becomes

---

[4] As the sun rises from the east, long shadows of things appear, extending towards the west. As the sun rises higher, shadows shorten until the sun settles in the middle of the sky. During this time, if the sunlight shines vertically, the shadows disappear. However, short shadows remain towards the south or north if its brightness is inclined. When the sun starts to incline towards the west, the shadows that disappeared begin to appear towards the east, or those that remained begin to stretch again towards the east, and at that time, it becomes the time for the Ẓuhr prayer. Additionally, midday [Ẓuhr], according to Islāmic law, is the midpoint between sunrise and sunset.

obligatory upon him to perform the ʿAṣr prayer at that time.

Timing of Maghrib and ʿIshāʾ Prayers

Issue 10: The time for Maghrib prayer extends from the moment the red twilight (which rises after sunset from the east) disappears from the sky until only enough time remains to perform the ʿIshāʾ prayer before midnight.

Issue 11: The time for ʿIshāʾ prayer extends from after the sufficient amount of time required to perform the Maghrib prayer after the onset of its time until midnight.

Issue 12: Midnight (for the Maghrib and ʿIshāʾ prayers) is the halfway point between sunset and the true dawn.

Issue 13: Each of the Maghrib and ʿIshāʾ prayers has a specific time and a shared time. The specific time for Maghrib prayer is the sufficient amount of time required to perform three units of prayer [rakʿats] when the sun sets, and the specific time for ʿIshāʾ prayer is the time required to perform it before midnight. The time interval between the specific time for Maghrib and the specific time for ʿIshāʾ is shared between Maghrib and ʿIshāʾ prayers.

Issue 14: If the specific time for ʿIshāʾ prayer begins and the person has not yet prayed Maghrib, it becomes obligatory for them to perform the ʿIshāʾ prayer at that time, then they perform Maghrib prayer.

Issue 15: If a person misses either the Maghrib or 'Ishā' prayer before midnight due to disobedience or for a legitimate excuse, then as an obligatory precaution, he must perform both prayers before dawn without the intention of fulfilling the duty [adā'] or making up for it [qaḍā'].

Rulings on the Timings of Prayer

Issue 16: In Islāmic law, it is recommended that a person offer a prayer as soon as its time frame begins. This is emphasized. If one cannot offer the prayer in its prime time, it is preferable to perform it at the time closest to that, unless delaying it is better for some reason, such as intending to join a congregation.

Issue 17: The worshiper must consider the horizon of their residence in determining the daily prayer times (even in regions close to the poles).

Issue 18: The Islāmically accountable individual [i.e., mukallaf] must ascertain the onset of prayer time or be assured to start praying. Alternatively, he can be informed that the time for prayer has begun by two just witnesses or by the call to prayer [adhān] from a trusted caller [mu'adhin] knowledgeable of the timings of prayer.

Issue 19: If one is certain that the time for prayer has come and begins praying but then has doubts during prayer regarding whether the time has come or not, his prayer becomes invalid. However, if he is certain that the prayer time has started during the prayer but doubts his past prayers, whether offered within the allotted time or beyond, his prayer remains valid.

Issue 20: If the Islāmically accountable individual [i.e., mukallaf] is assured of the onset of prayer time through media sources (that announce the Islāmic times) or similar means, he can commence the prayer.

Issue 21: If one is assured of the onset of prayer time while the call to prayer is being announced, he can pray and is not required to wait for the end of the call to prayer.[5]

Issue 22: If a creditor demands repayment of a debt during prayer time, and if the debtor can repay it, he must first repay the debt and then pray. Similarly, if another immediate obligation arises, prayer must be performed first in a situation with ample time for prayer. However, prayer must be performed first when the prayer time has become limited.

Issue 23: If the time for prayer has become limited such that performing recommended [mustaḥabbb] acts would cause some parts of the prayer to extend beyond its allotted time, performing those recommended acts is not permissible. For example, if performing Qunūt would lead

[5] As mentioned earlier regarding the Fajr prayer, observing precaution requires delaying it by approximately ten minutes after the Adhān begins.

to some parts of the prayer being performed outside its time, performing Qunūt is not permissible.

Issue 24: If one has enough time remaining to perform only one unit of prayer [rakʿat], he must pray with the intention of fulfilling the duty [adāʾ]. However, deliberately delaying the prayer until that time is not permissible.

Issue 25: If one has time remaining until sunset enough to perform five units of prayer, then he must pray Ẓuhr and ʿAṣr. If less than that remains, he must perform the ʿAṣr prayer (with the intention of fulfilling the duty) and make-up Ẓuhr. If time remains until midnight enough to perform only five units of prayer, then he must perform Maghrib and ʿIshāʾ. If less than that remains, he must offer ʿIshāʾ prayer only and then offer Maghrib. It is an obligatory precaution to perform it [Maghrib in this case] without the intention of fulfilling the duty [adāʾ] or making up for it [qaḍāʾ] but intending to perform what is due.

Issue 26: If a traveler has enough time remaining to perform three units of prayer before sunset, then he must pray Ẓuhr and ʿAṣr. If less than that remains, he must perform the ʿAṣr prayer and make-up Ẓuhr. If the remaining time until midnight is enough to perform only four units of prayer, he must perform Maghrib and ʿIshāʾ. If less than that is available, he must perform ʿIshāʾ only and then perform Maghrib without the intention of fulfillment or making up (with the intention of what is due) as a precaution. If one knows, after 'Ishā' prayer, that enough time remains to perform one or more units of prayer, he must immediately perform Maghrib with the intention of fulfilling the duty [adā'].

The Order of Prayers

Issue 27: It is obligatory to offer 'Aṣr prayer only after Ẓuhr, and likewise, it is obligatory to offer 'Ishā' prayer only after Maghrib. Deliberately performing these prayers out of this sequence invalidates them.

Issue 28: If the accountable person mistakenly or forgetfully performs the 'Aṣr prayer after Ẓuhr or the 'Ishā' prayer after Maghrib and then realizes his mistake after completing the prayer, his prayer is valid.

Issue 29: If one mistakenly starts the 'Aṣr prayer assuming he has prayed Ẓuhr and then realizes during the prayer that he has not prayed Ẓuhr if it is still within the overlapping time between Ẓuhr and 'Aṣr, then he must immediately correct his intention to Ẓuhr, complete it, then perform 'Aṣr. However, if it is within the specific time for Ẓuhr, it is preferable to correct his intention to Ẓuhr, complete it, and then perform both prayers in order.

Issue 30: If one mistakenly starts the 'Ishā' prayer assuming he has prayed Maghrib and then realizes during the prayer that he has not prayed Maghrib if it is still within the overlapping time between Maghrib and 'Ishā' and he has not begun the fourth unit of prayer [rak'at], he must immediately correct his intention to Maghrib, complete the prayer, then perform 'Ishā'. If he has already begun the fourth unit, completing the prayer and performing both prayers in order is preferable. Suppose it is within the specific time for Maghrib, and he has not begun the fourth unit. In that case, it is preferable to correct his intention to Maghrib, complete it, and then perform both prayers in order, considering the correct sequence.

Issue 31: If one starts praying with the intention of Ẓuhr and then remembers during the prayer that he has already prayed it, he cannot change his intention to 'Aṣr; rather, he must stop the prayer and perform 'Aṣr. Similarly, the same applies if one starts praying with the intention of Maghrib and then realizes during the prayer that he has already prayed it.

The Recommended Prayers

Issue 32: There are numerous recommended prayers (nawāfil). There has been a particular emphasis on the daily recommended prayers (both day and night prayers), especially the night prayer.

Issue 33: The daily nawāfil are the recommended prayers that the accountable person performs daily and night. Performing these prayers is highly important, and they are rewarded generously. Among these nawāfil prayers is the night prayer, which is prayed after midnight and has a special and unique significance among all recommended prayers. This prayer has numerous spiritual benefits, and Muslims should strive to perform it.

Issue 34: The daily recommended prayers [nawāfil] are as follows:

1. Ẓuhr Nafl [singular of nawāfil]: Eight units of prayer (four sets of two units each) before Ẓuhr prayer.

2. ʿAṣr Nafl: Eight units of prayer (four sets of two units each) before ʿAṣr prayer.

3. Maghrib Nafl: Four units of prayer (two sets of two units each) after Maghrib prayer.

4. ʿIshāʾ Nafl: Two units of prayer (sitting) after ʿIshāʾ prayer.[6]

5. Ṣubḥ Nafl: Two units of prayer before the Fajr prayer.

6. Night Nafl: Eleven units of prayer are to be offered between midnight and the dawn call to prayer [adhān]. (It is preferable to perform them in the last third of the night, and the closer to dawn, the greater their merit).

[6] Since the two units of prayer of ʿIshāʾ nafl are offered while sitting, they are counted as one unit; thus, the number of the prayer units of the daily recommended prayers is forty-three units (double the number of prayer units of the obligatory prayers).

Issue 35: On Friday, the combined number of units for Ẓuhr and ʿAṣr nawāfil is twenty, meaning an additional four units are added to the regular Ẓuhr and ʿAṣr nawāfil. There is no problem in performing them in the afternoon until sunset. However, it is preferable to perform the complete twenty units before the sun begins descending from its zenith [i.e., before Zawāl of the sun].

Issue 36: If the accountable person intends to perform the Ẓuhr and ʿAṣr nawāfil at their recommended time[7] but after the obligatory Ẓuhr and ʿAṣr prayers, then it is an obligatory precaution to offer them without the intention of fulfilling the duty [adā'] or making up for it [qaḍā'] (with the intention of fulfilling what is due).

Issue 37: The method of performing the night nafl prayer is as follows: Begin with four units, two by two, similar to the Fajr prayer, with the intention of "night prayer." Then, perform two units with the intention of "Shafʿ prayer," followed by one unit with the intention of "Witr prayer." It is recommended that during the Qunūt of the last unit, one seeks forgiveness, makes supplications for believers,

---

[7] The time for the Ẓuhr nafl prayer begins when the sun starts descending from its zenith up to when the shadow of an indicator or marker [such as a pole or stick] (formed after Ẓuhr) equals 2/7th of its length. For example, if the length of the indicator's shadow becomes two spans after Ẓuhr, the time for the Ẓuhr nafl prayer ends. As for the ʿAṣr nafl prayer, it extends until the length of the indicator's shadow (formed after Ẓuhr) reaches 4/7th of its length.

and asks God ﷻ for needs, as mentioned in supplication books.

Issue 38: Travelers, those facing difficulty performing the night prayer at its designated time, or those with valid excuses, such as the elderly or the sick, can perform the night prayer outside its designated time.

Issue 39: Reciting a Sūrah from the Qur'ān in the recommended prayers is not obligatory. Rather, reciting Sūrat al-Fātiḥah in each unit suffices, although reciting [another] Sūrah is also recommended.

Issue 40: The recommended prayers (except for the Witr prayer, which consists of one unit) are performed in sets of two units. It is permissible to offer them while sitting, although offering them while standing is preferable. If one performs them while sitting, it is recommended to count each set of two as one unit, except for the Watīrah prayer (the 'Ishā' nafl prayer), which is performed sitting as a precaution, not while standing.

Direction of Prayer

Issue 41: It is obligatory for the one praying to face the Ka'bah during his prayer, and for this reason, the direction of prayer is called the "Qiblah." As for those far away to the extent that they cannot truly face the Ka'bah, it is sufficient for them to pray in such a direction that it could be said that they are praying towards the Qiblah.

Issue 42: It is permissible to perform recommended prayers while walking or riding in transportation; in this case, it is not obligatory to face the Qiblah.

Issue 43: It is obligatory to face the Qiblah during the precautionary prayers and when making up for a missed tashahhud [testifying] and prostration. It is preferable as a precaution to face the Qiblah during prostrations of forgetfulness.

Issue 44: The one praying must ensure or ascertain the direction of the Qiblah, whether through a reliable compass or by the position of the sun[8] or stars (for those knowledgeable about them), or by other means. If unable to ascertain the direction, he should pray in the direction he believes is most likely correct, such as the direction indicated by the mosque's mihrab (prayer niche).

Issue 45: If one cannot find a way to determine the direction of the Qiblah and cannot be convinced of any direction, it is an obligatory precaution for him to pray

---

[8] It is said that on the 28th day of May and the 16th day of July of each year, the sun stands directly vertical over the Ka'bah at the moment it reaches its zenith, so that if we hold a marker or indicator (such as a wooden or iron pole) vertically to a flat ground, the direction of the shadow cast by the marker at the zenith, according to the horizon of Makkah (Mecca), is opposite to the Qibla (meaning the Qibla is in the direction opposite to where there is no shadow). Therefore, if this method ensures certainty about the Qibla direction, it is permissible to act according to it.

towards all four directions. If time does not allow for four prayers, he must repeat the prayer for the time available.

Issue 46: If the one praying initially confirmed the Qiblah direction and later found out he was mistaken, if the deviation from the Qiblah is less than about 90 degrees to the right or left, his prayer is valid. If he realizes the mistake during prayer, he must complete it while facing the Qibla. There is no distinction between having ample time or being pressed for time.

Issue 47: If one cannot ascertain the Qiblah direction, he acts based on his best estimate in all matters where facing the Qiblah is required, such as slaughtering animals and so on. If he cannot have a conviction about any direction and all directions seem equally correct to him, his action is valid regardless of the direction chosen.

Attire of the Praying Person

Issue 48: It is obligatory to cover the body during obligatory prayers and their follow-ups, such as precautionary prayers and making up missed parts, and it is an obligatory precaution to cover up [the body] during the prostrations of forgetfulness.

Issue 49: The obligation to cover in prayer is not limited to the presence of non-maḥrams [a person one can and is allowed to marry] in the place of prayer; rather, covering is a condition for the validity of prayer even if no one is present.

Issue 50: A man must cover his private parts during prayer, even if no one sees him, and it is preferable to cover his body from his navel to his knees as well.

Issue 51: A woman must cover her entire body and hair during prayer, except the area of her face washed during ablution, the hands up to the wrists, and the feet up to the ankles. However, in the presence of a non-maḥram, it is also obligatory to cover up the feet.

Issue 52: The chin is part of the face, so it is not obligatory for a woman to cover it during prayer. However, the area below the chin (the lower part of the chin) is not considered part of the face and must be covered.

Issue 53: Covering is not obligatory in funeral prayer, but observing it is recommended.

Issue 54: Covering is a condition for the validity of recommended prayers, just as obligatory prayers.

Issue 55: If the accountable person realizes during prayer that there is something amiss in the obligatory covering, it is preferable to complete the prayer and repeat it. However, if he immediately rectifies the covering, his prayer remains valid. Similarly, if he realizes after the prayer that he did not observe the obligatory covering, his prayer remains valid.

Conditions for the Attire of the Praying Person

Issue 56: The following conditions are required for the attire of the praying person:

1. Purity

2. Permissibility

3. Not being made of parts of a carcass [of an animal that has not been slaughtered according to Islāmic law]

4. Not being made of parts of an animal whose flesh is not permissible to eat

5. Not being made of gold for men

6. Not being pure silk for men

Purity

Issue 57: The praying person's attire and body must be pure [ṭāhir; clean].

Issue 58: If someone is unaware that praying with an impure body or garment invalidates the prayer, and he prays while his body or garment is impure, his prayer is invalid, except if he is unaware or an inculpable ignorant,[9]

[9] An inculpable ignorant [jāhil qāṣir] is unaware of or knows of his ignorance but cannot find a way out of it.

such that he does not even consider the possibility that praying with an impure body or garment invalidates the prayer.

Issue 59: If someone did not know that his body or garment was impure and noticed that his prayer remains valid after the prayer. However, if he had been aware of the impurity beforehand and had forgotten and prayed with it, his prayer would have been invalid.

Issue 60: If someone doubts whether his garment is impure, he should base his judgment on the assumption that it is pure and his prayer with it is valid. However, if his garment became impure beforehand and he doubts whether it has been purified or not, his prayer in this garment is not valid.

Issue 61: If someone did not know whether his body or garment was pure or impure and he prayed, then later discovered that either was impure, his prayer remains valid.

Issue 62: If someone notices during prayer and realizes that his body or garment is impure, and he knows that the impurity was there beforehand if he has ample time, then his prayer is invalidated, and he must repeat it after purification. However, in the case of limited time, if purification of the body or garment, or changing or removing the garment, is possible without disrupting the form of the prayer, he should do so during the prayer and continue praying. But if these actions necessitate disrupting the form of the prayer, he should complete his prayer in that condition, and his prayer is valid.

Issue 63: If someone purifies his garment, becomes certain of its purity, and prays with it, then notices after the prayer and realizes that it was not properly purified, his prayer is valid, but he must purify it for subsequent prayers.

Instances where the purity of the praying person's body or garment is not obligatory:

Issue 64: Prayer is valid with an impure body or garment in the four following cases:

First Case: Blood from Wounds and Sores

Issue 65: If there is blood from a wound or sore on the praying person's body or garment, and purifying the body or garment or changing the garment is difficult and causes hardship or inconvenience to oneself or others, then one may pray with it as long as the wound or sore has not healed. Similarly, prayer is valid with pus that oozes out with blood and medicine applied to the wound, which becomes impure.

Issue 66: This ruling does not apply to wounds that heal quickly and are easily purified. Prayer with such wounds is invalid.

Issue 67: If a part of the body or garment gets soiled with moisture from a wound, extending beyond the usual extent of wound moisture, there is no problem praying with it. However, if a part of the body or garment far from the wound becomes soiled due to the contact with the wound's moisture, and one prays with it, his prayer is invalid.

Issue 68: If there are several wounds on the body close to each other to the extent that they count as one wound, there is no problem in praying with the resulting blood as long as all of them have not healed. However, suppose they are separated to the extent that each counts as a separate wound. Whenever one of them heals, it is necessary to purify it along with the adjacent part of the garment for the sake of prayer.

Issue 69: If the worshiper becomes certain that the blood on his body or garment is excusable, such as being certain that it is from a wound or sore, and later realizes after the prayer that it is not excusable, his prayer is valid.

Second Case: Blood Less Than the Size of a Fingertip

Issue 70: If there is blood on the praying person's body or garment other than that mentioned previously,[10] and its size is less than the size of a fingertip (considering the following conditions), there is no problem in praying with

[10] That is blood from a wound or sore, which is troublesome to purify.

it. However, if it is the size of a fingertip or more, prayer with it is invalid.

Issue 71: The validity of prayer with blood less than the size of a fingertip is conditioned by:

1. It should not be menstrual blood, as prayer with it on the body or garment is invalid, regardless of the amount. Applying the same ruling to postpartum and irregular bleeding is an obligatory precaution.

2. It should not be from the blood of impure animals (like dogs and pigs), the blood of animals whose flesh is unlawful to eat, or the blood of a disbelieving person.

3. It should not come into contact with external moisture unless mixed with it and absorbed without exceeding the excusable limit. In this case, prayer is valid with it; otherwise, it is not valid as an obligatory precaution.

Issue 72: If the body or garment does not get stained with blood but the impurity transfers to it, such as when the hands or garment are wet and become impure [najis] by contact with dry blood without transferring the blood itself, then prayer with such impurity is not valid even if the extent of impurity is less than the size of a fingertip.

Issue 73: If the blood is removed from the body or garment but the place is not purified, and its size is less than the size of a fingertip, then prayer with it is valid.

Issue 74: If blood falls on a garment with a lining or falls on the lining and reaches the garment, and if the total amount of blood on the garment and lining is less than the size of a fingertip, then prayer with it is valid. However, if it is the size of a fingertip or more, prayer with it is invalid.

Third Case: Impurity of Garments That Prayer Is Not Valid With

Issue 75: If small garments that do not suffice to cover the private parts, such as socks, gloves, and stockings, as well as items like rings and bracelets, become impure by contact with impurity, prayer is valid with them.

Issue 76: If the praying person carries impure items such as handkerchiefs, keys, or knives, praying with them is no problem.

Fourth Case: Wearing Impure Garment Out of Necessity

Issue 77: If someone is forced to pray while his body or garment is in a state of impurity due to extreme cold, lack of water, or similar reasons, his prayer is valid.

Permissibility

Issue 78: The garment of the worshiper must be permissible for use [mubaḥ], meaning that it must not be usurped [maghsub; obtained by unlawful means—whether stolen from someone or bought with money with which khums or zakāt, when obligatory, were not given].

Issue 79: If someone is ignorant of the prohibition of wearing a usurped garment, his prayer is valid. However, suppose he knowingly prayed with it despite being aware of its prohibition. In that case, he must repeat the prayer with a garment permissible for use, even if he was unaware that it invalidated it.

Issue 80: If someone is unaware that his garment is usurped or forgets about it and prays with it, his prayer is valid.

Issue 81: If someone intentionally prays with a garment containing usurped threads, buttons, or similar items, his prayer is invalid.

Not being made of parts of a carcass [of an animal that has not been slaughtered according to Islāmic law]

Issue 82: The garment of the worshiper must not consist of parts of a dead animal whose blood gushes out [e.g., cow, chicken, etc.], and it is an obligatory precaution that it also does not consist of parts of a dead animal whose blood does not gush out [e.g., fish, mosquito, etc.].

Issue 83: If the worshiper carries parts of an animal carcass, his prayer is invalid as an obligatory precaution. However, if what is carried consists of parts that do not decay, such as hair, wool, horns, or bones, from animals whose flesh is permissible [to eat], it does not harm the validity of the prayer.

Issue 84: Imported hides [animal skin] of animals whose flesh is permissible from non-Muslim countries and those with doubtful purification via ritual slaughter practices [tazkiyah],[11] are not considered the same as carcasses in terms of purity and impurity. They are considered pure, but praying with them (e.g., wearing clothes of such animal skin) is invalid. However, if the accountable person prayed with them in the past out of ignorance of the ruling, his prayer is valid. Similarly, suppose the importer is a Muslim, and he may have inspected them in terms of purification

---

[11] The term *tazkiyah* [purification via ritual slaughter] refers to the conditions set by Islām for meat to become ritually pure or permissible. Tazkiyah, in the case of animals whose flesh is permissible for consumption, refers to the conditions that make the animal's parts ritually pure and allow the consumption of its meat. For animals whose flesh is not permissible for consumption, it refers to the conditions that render their parts ritually pure. The methods of tazkiyah are as follows:

a. in case of animals other than the camel, slaughtering by way of severing the animal's windpipe and the two jugular veins [*thabḥ*],
b. in case of the camel, slaughtering by way of piercing it with a knife or by any other sharp instrument in its breastplate, where depression is found at the lower part of the neck [*naḥr*], and
c. hunting for wild animals.

via ritual slaughter. In that case, there is no issue in praying with them.

Not being made of parts of an animal whose flesh is not permissible to eat

Issue 85: It is necessary that the garment of the praying person not be made from parts of an animal whose flesh is not permissible to eat. The presence of even a single hair from such an animal on the body or garment of the praying person invalidates the prayer.

Issue 86: If there is pure moisture on the body or garment of the praying person, such as saliva or nasal discharge from an animal whose flesh is not permissible to eat, such as a cat, then his prayer is invalid unless the impurity is removed after drying. Prayer also becomes invalid if the secretion of a bird whose flesh is not permissible to eat is found on the body or garment of the praying person. However, the prayer is valid if it is removed from the garment or body after drying.

Issue 87: There is no problem in praying while having human hair, sweat, saliva, wax, honey, pearls, or shells on the garment or body of the praying person.

Issue 88: Prayer with a garment that the accountable person suspects to be made from parts of an animal whose flesh is or is not permissible to eat is valid.

Not being made of gold for men

Issue 89: Wearing a garment woven with gold or containing it is forbidden for men and invalidates the prayer. However, women have no problem in all circumstances (during prayer or otherwise).

Issue 90: It is forbidden for a man to wear a necklace, ring, or watch made of gold even for a short period (for example, while enjoining the marriage contract), even if he does not intend it as adornment for himself and conceals it from others. It is also an obligatory precaution that prayers with such items are invalid.

Issue 91: A man using gold in surgical operations for bones and dental treatment is not prohibited, and it does not invalidate the prayer.

Issue 92: What is called white gold, if it is made from the same yellow gold but whitened due to mixing, has the same ruling as yellow gold. However, if the quantity of gold is small to the extent that it can no longer be referred to as gold, then there is no problem with its use for men. There is also no problem with wearing platinum.

Issue 93: If a man prays wearing a ring or garment made of gold out of ignorance or forgetfulness, his prayer is valid.

Not being pure silk for men

Issue 94: If the garment of the praying man (even regarding clothing that is insufficient to cover his private parts such as a turban, socks, and the like) is made of pure silk, then the prayer with it is invalid, and wearing it even outside of prayer is prohibited. However, if he carries a silk handkerchief, for example, in his pocket, there is no problem with that, and it does not harm the validity of the prayer.

Issue 95: If the garment's lining—even if it is only a part of it—is made of pure silk, then it is not permissible to wear it, and prayer with it is not valid.

Issue 96: There is no problem with wearing a garment only suspected to be made of pure silk or otherwise, and prayer is valid with it.

Issue 97: A woman wearing a silk garment in prayer or outside of it is not a problem.

What Is Recommended and What Is Detestable in Terms of the Prayer Garment

Issue 98: Among the recommendations [mustaḥabb] for the prayer garment are as follows: the garment should be white and made of cotton or linen, and one should wear his cleanest clothes, use perfume, and wear a ʿaqīq [agate] ring.

Issue 99: Among the detestable [makrūḥ] aspects of the prayer garment are as follows: wearing a black, dirty, or tight-fitting garment, wearing the garment of someone who drinks alcohol or someone who does not guard against impurity, wearing a garment with images of living beings, even underwear, wearing an unbuttoned garment or a ring with an image on it.

Conditions for the Place of Prayer

Several conditions must be met for the place of prayer:

Permissibility

Issue 100: The prayer area must be permissible for use [mubaḥ], meaning that it must not be usurped or forcibly occupied [maghsub; obtained by unlawful means—whether seized from someone without permission or consent or bought with money with which khums or zakāt, when obligatory, were not given].

Issue 101: Praying on a usurped carpet or bed is invalid, even if the ground beneath it is permissible. Similarly, praying on a permissible carpet spread on the usurped ground is also invalid.

Issue 102: The prayer is valid if someone prays in a place he does not know or forgets it is usurped.

Issue 103: If someone is aware of the usurpation of a place but is unaware that praying in a usurped place is invalid, and he prays there, then his prayer is invalid.

Issue 104: If someone shares ownership of a property with another person, and if his share is not separate from his partner's share, he cannot pray in that property without the partner's consent.

Issue 105: Prayer is invalid in a property that benefits someone else without their permission. For example, in a rented house, if the owner or someone else wishes to pray in that house without the current tenant's permission, their prayer is invalid.

Stability

Issue 106: The place of prayer must be stable, meaning the worshiper should be able to perform prayer there in tranquility without disturbance. Therefore, it is not valid to pray in places that warrant movement of the body without choice, such as in a moving car or train or on some springy beds, except in cases of necessity to pray in such a place due to limited time or similar circumstances.

Issue 107: Travelers in public transportation who fear missing the prayer must ask the driver to stop, and the driver must respond. If the driver does not stop for any reason, the travelers must pray. At the same time, the vehicle is in motion, taking into account the direction of the Qiblah and performing the standing, bowing, and prostration of prayer as much as possible.

Not to be from what prohibits staying in it

Issue 108: It is required for the place of prayer not to be from what prohibits staying in it, such as places where human life is exposed to serious danger, as well as places upon which standing or sitting is prohibited, such as a rug on which the name of God or Qur'ānic verses are written in a way that standing on it is considered a violation of its sanctity.

Not to be ahead of the grave of the Prophet ﷺ and the Imām ؑ

Issue 109: It is necessary for the praying person not to stand ahead of the grave of the Prophet ﷺ and the Imām ؑ in such a way that warrants turning his back to the grave while praying. However, there is no problem in being at the same level.

Issue 110: If there is a wall between the praying person and the sacred grave so that standing in front of it is not considered disrespectful, then praying is no problem. However, the sacred shrine, lattice enclosure of the tomb [ḍarīḥ], or the cloth placed over it would not be sufficient to discount any disrespectful behavior toward them.

Purity of the place of prostration

Issue 111: It is necessary for the area where the forehead touches the ground during prostration to be pure. However, suppose the place where the person is praying is impure except for the area where the forehead touches the ground. The impurity does not transfer to the body or the clothes of the praying person. There is no problem in that case, and the prayer is valid.

Considering the distance between a man and a woman

Issue 112: It is an obligatory precaution that the distance between a man and a woman during prayer (outside the Sacred Mosque in Makkah) be at least one span. In this case, their prayers are valid whether the woman stands beside the man or ahead of him, and there is no distinction in this regard between those who are lawful to marry [non-maḥram] and those who are not [maḥram].

Being level

Issue 113: It is obligatory that the area where the forehead touches the ground during prayer not be higher or lower than the area where the knees and the tips of the toes touch the ground by more than the width of four joined fingers.

Issue 114: It is recommended [mustaḥabb] to pray in the following places:

1. Mosques (the best of which is the Sacred Mosque in Makkah, followed by the Prophet's ﷺ Mosque, then the Mosque of Kūfah, and al-Aqṣa Mosque, followed by the congregational mosque in any land).

2. Shrines of the Imāms ﷺ—offering prayers at the sacred shrines is better than in mosques.

3. The sanctified sanctuaries of the Prophets ﷺ and the shrines of the friends of God, the righteous, and the scholars (may God be pleased with them).

Rulings of the Mosque

Issue 115: It is prohibited to sully the ground, ceiling, walls, and roof of the mosque with impurity. If impurity occurs, it is obligatory to purify it promptly.

Issue 116: The ritual purification of the mosque is a collective obligation.[12] Its obligation is not limited to those who caused its impurity but extends to all capable of purifying it.

---

[12] The collective obligation (*al-wājib al-kifā'ī*)—in contrast to the individual obligation (*al-wājib al-'aynī*)—refers to the duty that some individuals must initiate. However, if they perform it, it exempts the rest; if no one performs it, all are considered sinful. Examples of such obligations include purifying the mosque and washing and burying the deceased. On the other hand, the individual obligation is the duty that is individually obligatory upon each accountable person, such as daily prayers, alms tax, and almsgiving.

Issue 117: It is prohibited to sully the sacred sanctuaries of the Imāms عليهم السلام with impurity. If impurity occurs and remaining in such a state of impurity is considered an insult, it is obligatory to purify it. Otherwise, purification is commendable.

Issue 118: Decorating mosques with gold is considered extravagant and prohibited. Otherwise, it is detestable.

Issue 119: The mosque's status and sanctity must be respected. Therefore, actions conflicting with its dignity and status should be avoided.

Issue 120: Engaging in certain activities, such as educational classes, is permissible in mosques as long as they do not conflict with the mosque's dignity and do not interfere with congregational prayers and the worshipers.

Issue 121: The mosque's destruction or any part of it is not permissible except for a compelling reason or interest that cannot be overcome or neglected.

Issue 122: If a mosque is seized or demolished and replaced by something else, or if its features as a mosque have diminished due to abandonment, and there is no hope of rebuilding it, it is not unlawful to make it impure [najis], but it is recommended precaution not to do so.

Issue 123: If a mosque falls within the municipal plan for reconstruction in a street, and the necessity arises to demolish part of it, with no hope of restoration to how it was, it does not fall under the legal rulings of a mosque.

Issue 124: Establishing a museum or library and the like in the corner of the mosque hall is not permissible if it contradicts the sanctity of the mosque hall or requires alterations to its structure.

Issue 125: If a movable and unstable structure is designated as a mosque, such as a means of transportation, it is an obligatory precaution to validate its legal status as a mosque, and it is thus made subject to the rulings of a mosque.

Issue 126: It is recommended [mustaḥabb] to clean and maintain the mosque. Moreover, it is recommended that those intending to visit the mosque perfume themselves, wear clean and elegant clothes, ensure their shoes or feet are not sullied with impurity or filth, hurry to enter the mosque before others and stay behind to leave after them, and engage in much remembrance of God and feel awe and humility in their hearts upon entering and leaving. It is also recommended to pray two units of prayer upon entering the mosque with the intention of greeting it. These two units of prayer can be substituted with offering obligatory or recommended prayers.

Issue 127: Sleeping in the mosque is detestable [makrūḥ].

Issue 128: Temporary shelters and Ḥusayniyyahs are not subject to the rulings of a mosque.

Adhān and Iqāmah

Issue 129: It is recommended [mustaḥabb] to perform the Adhān [call to prayer] and Iqāmah [second call to prayer] before the obligatory daily prayers. This recommendation is particularly emphasized in the Fajr and Maghrib prayers, especially when performed in congregation. However, Adhān and Iqāmah are not prescribed for other obligatory prayers such as the Ṣalāt al-Āyāt [Prayer of the Signs].

Issue 130: The Adhān consists of eighteen phrases in the following order:

- "Allāhu Akbar" (God is the Greatest): four times
- "Ash-hadu an lā ilāha illa Allāh" (I bear witness that there is no god but God): twice
- "Ash-hadu anna Muḥammadan Rasūl Allāh" (I bear witness that Muḥammad is the Messenger of God): twice
- "Ḥayya ʿala aṣ-Ṣalāt" (Hasten to prayer): twice
- "Ḥayya ʿala al-Falāḥ" (Hasten to deliverance): twice

- "Ḥayya 'ala Khayr al-'Amal" (Hasten to the best of deeds): twice

- "Allāhu Akbar" [God is the Greatest]: twice

- "Lā ilāha illa Allāh" (There is no god but God): twice

Iqāmah is similar to Adhān but differs in that "Allāhu Akbar" (God is the Greatest) is recited twice at the beginning, and "Qad Qāmat aṣ-Ṣalāt" (the prayer has been established) is added twice after "Ḥayya 'ala Khayr al-'Amal" (hasten to the best of deeds) and "Lā ilāha illa Allāh" (there is no god but God) is recited only once at the end.

Issue 131: Reciting the phrase "Ash-hadu anna 'Alīyyan Walīyyullāh" (I bear witness that 'Alī is the Vicegerent of God) as a slogan of Shī'īsm is good and important, but it is not part of Adhān and Iqāmah. It must be recited with the intention of seeking nearness to God.

Issue 132: Broadcasting the Adhān (which is raised to announce the time of prayer) and hearing it by the listeners are confirmed recommendations [mustaḥabb acts].

Issue 133: There is no objection to broadcasting the Adhān from mosques and other places through loudspeakers in the usual and common manner to announce the time of prayer. However, it is not permissible to broadcast Qur'ānic verses, supplications, and the like if it annoys neighbors.

Issue 134: If someone intends to join a congregation for which the Adhān and Iqāmah have already been recited, it is not recommended for him to recite the Adhān and Iqāmah for his prayer.

Issue 135: It is recommended for a person to stand facing the Qiblah during the Adhān, having performed partial-body ablution [wuḍū']or major ablution [ghusl], and to place his hands beside his ears, raise and elongate his voice leave short intervals between the phrases of the Adhān, and refrain from speaking during it.

Issue 136: It is recommended for a person to maintain tranquility during the Iqāmah, with its recitation being quieter than the Adhān. The phrases of the Iqāmah should not be joined together, although the intervals between them should not be as long as those between the phrases of the Adhān.

Issue 137: It is recommended for a person to sit briefly between the Adhān and Iqāmah or to prostrate, glorify God, remain silent for a while, speak, or perform two voluntary units of prayer.

Obligatory Acts of Prayer

Issue 138: The obligatory acts of prayer are eleven:

1. Intention

2. Standing [Qiyām]

3. Takbīrat al-Iḥrām—the "opening takbīr": saying "Allāhu Akbar" (God is the Greatest), signifying the beginning of the prayer

4. Recitation [of Qur'ānic Sūrahs]

5. Bowing [Rukū']

6. Prostration [Sujūd]

7. Dhikr [Remembrance of God]

8. Testifying [tashahhud; reciting the shahādah]

9. Salutation [Taslīm]

10. Sequence [Tartīb]

11. Close Succession [Muwālāt]

The following issues will discuss the details of these obligations and their rulings.

Issue 139: Some of the obligatory acts of prayer are classified as "pillars" [rukn], meaning that their addition or omission invalidates the prayer, even if it was due to forgetfulness or inadvertence. Others are classified as "non-pillars" (ghayr rukn), meaning that intentionally adding or omitting them invalidates the prayer, while unintentional omissions do not harm its validity.

Issue 140: The pillars of prayer are as follows:

1. Intention

2. Takbīrat al-Iḥrām

3. Standing during Takbīrat al-Iḥrām and before bowing (the standing connected to the bowing)

4. Bowing

5. The two prostrations

Intention

Issue 141: Intention (one of the pillar obligations) is the resolve to perform the prayer in compliance with the command of God ﷻ.

Issue 142: It is not obligatory to articulate the intention, such as saying: "I intend to pray four units of prayer as the Ẓuhr prayer, seeking nearness to God ﷻ." Likewise, there is no requirement for a formal announcement or declaration of intention in the mind or heart; it suffices to intend to perform the act in compliance with the Divine command.

Issue 143: The praying person must know the specific prayer he intends to perform. Therefore, if, for example, one intends to perform four units of prayer without specifying whether it is Ẓuhr or ʿAṣr, his prayer becomes invalid.

Issue 144: A person must offer the prayer solely with the intention of obeying the command of God ﷻ. Therefore, if one performs the prayer to show off and ostentation [riyāʾ]—that is, to pretend to be religious and the like—he has sinned, and his prayer is invalid.

Issue 145: If the praying person performs certain parts of the prayer to show off [ostentation], repeating those parts is an obligatory precaution.

Issue 146: If a person leaves out a recommended part of the prayer intending to remedy ostentation in his prayer, his action is not considered ostentation, and his prayer is valid.

Issue 147: Switching his intention from one prayer to another[13] is not permissible except in special circumstances. Sometimes, switching is obligatory, and in other cases, it is recommended.[14]

Issue 148: Circumstances where switching intention from one prayer to another is obligatory are as follows:

---

[13] That is, during the prayer.

[14] Cases where such switching is permissible are mentioned in the detailed books.

1. From the prayer to the Ẓuhr prayer before the ʿAṣr prayer time begins, if one remembers during the prayer that he has not yet prayed Ẓuhr.

2. From the ʿIshāʾ prayer to the Maghrib prayer before the ʿIshāʾ prayer time begins, if one remembers during the ʿIshāʾ prayer that he has not yet prayed Maghrib, provided he has not yet passed the point where switching is allowed, i.e., before entering the bowing position of the fourth unit.

3. From one make-up [qaḍāʾ] prayer to another make-up prayer, the order between them is considered. For example, making up missed Ẓuhr and ʿAṣr prayers for one day if one starts the second prayer before beginning the first one due to forgetfulness.

Standing [Qiyām]

Issue 149: Known as Qiyām, standing at the beginning of the prayer when Takbīrat al-Iḥrām is recited and also before proceeding with bowing is a pillar. Therefore, omitting it invalidates the prayer, even if done unintentionally or due to forgetfulness.

Issue 150: Standing during recitation [of Sūrat al-Fātiḥah and the other chapter] and the four tasbīḥs [the glorifications recited in the third and fourth units of prayer], as well as standing after bowing, is obligatory but not a pillar. Deliberately omitting it invalidates the prayer, while unintentional omission does not affect its validity.

Issue 151: A person capable of offering prayer while standing must stand from the beginning of the prayer until the bowing—when a valid excuse does not apply. Additionally, standing after bowing and before going into prostration is obligatory.

Issue 152: If one forgets to bow and sits after reciting Sūrat al-Fātiḥah and the other chapter, remember that during this time, he must return to the standing position and then bow. His prayer becomes invalid if he returns directly to the bowing position without standing up and straightening his back.

Issue 153: While standing, the worshiper must maintain stillness, stand upright without leaning significantly in any direction, and refrain from leaning on anything unless necessary due to constraint, forgetfulness, or unintentional movement.

Issue 154: During the recitation of Sūrat al-Fātiḥah and the other chapter, or the four tasbīḥs in the third and fourth units, the worshiper's body must remain steady. If he intends to move slightly forward or backward or shift his body slightly to the right or left, he must pause his current recitation during the movement.

Issue 155: When one is standing [i.e., during Qiyām], it is recommended to stand erect, with the shoulders slightly lowered, placing the palms on the thighs, fingers joined together, looking at the place of prostration, distributing the body weight evenly on both feet, maintaining humility and reverence, and aligning the feet side by side.

Issue 156: If one cannot stand during prayer, he may pray sitting. However, if he can stand with support [e.g., leaning on something], it is thus obligatory for him to pray standing.

Issue 157: If one prays while sitting, he must stand whenever possible without experiencing hardship or difficulty. Therefore, if one can stand for some units and parts of the prayer but not the entire prayer, then he must pray standing to the extent of his capability. When unable to stand, he should complete the prayer sitting. If the ability to stand returns, he should resume standing and complete the prayer in that position.

Issue 158: If one cannot stand for the prayer but can stand for the time needed to make Takbīrat al-Iḥrām, he must start the prayer standing and then complete the remainder of the prayer sitting. Similarly, if his ability to stand returns after reciting Sūrat al-Fātiḥah and the other chapter, he must bow from a standing position.

Issue 159: If one can pray standing but fears illness or harm due to standing, he may pray sitting. He may pray lying down if he has the same fear while sitting.

Issue 160: If one cannot pray sitting, he must pray lying down. It is preferable for him to lie on their right side, facing the Qiblah with his face and body, but if he cannot, he may lie on his left side in the same manner. If lying on his side is not possible, he should lie on his back, facing the Qiblah with the soles of his feet.

Issue 161: If one prays lying down but can stand or sit during the prayer without hardship, difficulty, or harm, he must transition to standing or sitting to the best of his ability.

Issue 162: If one cannot stand for prayer due to an excuse but will likely be able to stand later towards the end of the prayer's interval of time, it is an obligatory precaution for him to wait until he can stand. However, if he offers the prayer sitting at its prime time due to an excuse and the excuse persists until the end of its time, his prayer is valid, and there is no obligation to repeat it.

Issue 163: If one cannot offer the prayer standing at its prime time, knowing he will not be able to do so until the end of its time either, he may offer the prayer sitting at its prime time. However, he must repeat the prayer if he can stand before it ends.

Takbīrat al-Iḥrām [The "Opening Takbīr"]

Issue 164: Takbīrat al-Iḥrām is obligatory in prayer. It means saying "Allāhu Akbar" (God is the Greatest) at the beginning of the prayer.

Issue 165: Omitting Takbīrat al-Iḥrām at the beginning of the prayer invalidates the prayer, whether done intentionally or unintentionally. Similarly, if one performs it correctly at the beginning of the prayer and then says "Allāhu Akbar" again with the same intention after a short period (not reaching the extent of disrupting the close succession[15]), or without a divide, his prayer becomes invalid, intentionally or inadvertently.

Issue 166: It is obligatory to pronounce Takbīrat al-Iḥrām audibly in a way that can be heard by oneself if there is no hearing impairment and no noise in the surrounding environment prevents hearing it.

Issue 167: Takbīrat al-Iḥrām must be pronounced in correct Arabic wording. Its translation into Persian or pronouncing it with vocalization is invalid (such as pronouncing the letter "h" in the name of God with an open sound).

Issue 168: When pronouncing Takbīrat al-Iḥrām, one must ensure composure and stillness of the body. If one

---

[15] See Issue 303 for the meaning of close succession.

performs the Takbīrat al-Iḥrām intentionally and voluntarily in motion, his prayer becomes invalid.

Issue 169: Whoever does not know how to pronounce the Takbīrat al-Iḥrām must learn it.

Issue 170: If one doubts whether he has performed Takbīrat al-Iḥrām or not, and the doubt arises before starting with the remembrance of God [dhikr] or recitation [of Sūrat al-Fātiḥah and the other chapter], he must perform it. However, if the doubt arises after starting with Sūrat al-Fātiḥah or even seeking refuge in God, he should ignore his doubt and continue his prayer.

Issue 171: If one doubts whether he has correctly performed Takbīrat al-Iḥrām after performing it, he should not pay attention to his doubt.

Recitation

Issue 172: In the first and second units of the obligatory daily prayers, it is obligatory to recite Sūrat al-Fātiḥah first, and it is an obligatory precaution to recite another complete Sūrah after it.

Issue 173: Recitation is obligatory but not a pillar of the prayer, meaning that deliberately omitting it invalidates it, while unintentional or forgetful omission does not affect its validity.

Issue 174: If the time for prayer becomes limited, it is obligatory to skip the recitation of the other Sūrah.

Issue 175: If one inadvertently recites a Sūrah before Sūrat al-Fātiḥah and remembers before bowing, he should repeat it after reciting Sūrat al-Fātiḥah. However, if he remembers during the recitation of the other Sūrah, he should stop reciting it and, after reciting Sūrat al-Fātiḥah, start the other Sūrah again.

Issue 176: If he forgets to recite Sūrat al-Fātiḥah and the other Sūrah or one of them and remembers after entering the bowing position, his prayer is valid.

Issue 177: If he remembers before going into bowing that he did not recite Sūrat al-Fātiḥah and the other Sūrah or only the other Sūrah, he should make up for what he missed and then bow down. If he remembers that he only missed Sūrat al-Fātiḥah, he should recite it first and then repeat the other Sūrah afterward. Similarly, suppose he bends forward to bow down and remembers before reaching the full bowing position that he missed Sūrat al-Fātiḥah and the other Sūrah, or both. In that case, he should return to the standing position and make up for what he missed, following what has been mentioned earlier in this ruling.

Issue 178: In obligatory prayers, it is not permissible for him to recite any of the Sūrahs that contain an obligatory sajdah [prostration]. Based on obligatory precaution, if he intentionally or inadvertently recites one of them and reaches the verse that contains the obligatory sajdah, he must perform the prostration of recitation, then rise and complete the Sūrah if it has not been finished, complete the prayer, then repeat it. If he realizes that before reaching the verse that contains the obligatory sajdah, then it is an obligatory precaution for him to stop reciting the Sūrah, recite another one, and after completing the prayer, repeat it.

Issue 179: If he hears the verse that contains the obligatory sajdah during the prayer, his prayer is valid. After hearing the verse that contains the obligatory sajdah, he must nod instead of performing the prostration and continue his prayer.

Issue 180: If he begins reciting Sūrat al-Ikhlāṣ or Sūrat al-Kāfirūn after Sūrat al-Fātiḥah, it is not permissible for him to stop reciting it and switch to another Sūrah. However, in the Friday prayer, if he forgets and starts reciting one of them instead of Sūrat al-Jumuʿah and Sūrat al-Munāfiqūn, it is permissible for him to stop reciting it and instead recite Sūrat al-Jumuʿah and Sūrat al-Munāfiqūn.

Issue 181: If he recites a Sūrah other than Sūrat al-Ikhlāṣ or Sūrat al-Kāfirūn in prayer, as long as he has not passed halfway through it, it is permissible for him to stop reciting it and switch to another Sūrah.

Issue 182: If he forgets a portion of the Sūrah he is reciting in prayer or is unable to complete it due to lack of time or another compelling reason, he must leave it and recite another Sūrah instead, whether he has passed halfway through it or not, and whether the Sūrah he was reciting is one of Sūrat al-Ikhlāṣ or Sūrat al-Kāfirūn or not.

Issue 183: Reciting another Sūrah is not obligatory in the recommended prayers (nawāfil), even if a vow made the recommended prayer obligatory. However, in some recommended prayers where a specific Sūrah is mentioned, such as the prayer for parents, if one intends to recite it in the prescribed manner, he must recite the same Sūrah.

Issue 184: In the third and fourth units of obligatory prayers, reciting the four tasbīhs [glorifications] (Subḥānallāh, Alḥamdulillāh, Lā ilāha illallāh, Allāhu Akbar) once is sufficient, although it is recommended precaution to repeat them three times, and reciting Sūrat al-Fātiḥah instead of them is also acceptable.

Issue 185: If one recites the four tasbīhs but does not know how often he has done so, there is no obligation upon him. However, if he has not entered the bowing position, he can assume the least number and repeat them until he is certain about completing them thrice.

Issue 186: If one is accustomed to reciting the four tasbīhs, usually in the third and fourth units of prayer, and intends to recite Sūrat al-Fātiḥah instead but accidentally recites the tasbīhs as usual, his prayer is valid. Similarly, if one is accustomed to reciting Sūrat al-Fātiḥah usually and intends to recite the tasbīhs instead but accidentally recites Sūrat al-Fātiḥah, his prayer is valid.

Issue 187: If one recites the Sūrat al-Fātiḥah and another Sūrah in the third or fourth units of prayer inadvertently or thinking that he is in the first or second unit and remembers while bowing or after that, his prayer is valid.

Issue 188: If doubt arises while standing whether or not he recited Sūrat al-Fātiḥah or the four tasbīhs, then it is obligatory that he recite one of them. But if doubt arises regarding reciting the four tasbīhs while uttering the recommended istighfār [asking forgiveness] before bowing, then it is not obligatory for him to recite them.

Issue 189: While bowing in the third or fourth unit, if he doubts whether he recited Sūrat al-Fātiḥah or the four tasbīhs, he does not need to concern himself with his doubt. But suppose doubt arises while bending forward to bow and before reaching the full bowing position. In that case, it is an obligatory precaution for him to return to the standing position and recite Sūrat al-Fātiḥah or the four tasbīhs.

Issue 190: Men must recite Sūrat al-Fātiḥah and the other Sūrah aloud [jahr] in the first two units of Fajr, Maghrib, and 'Ishā' prayers, while both men and women should recite them in a whisper [ikhfāt] in Ẓuhr and 'Aṣr prayers.

Issue 191: A woman can choose between reciting Sūrat al-Fātiḥah and the other Sūrah aloud or in a whisper in Fajr, Maghrib, and 'Ishā' prayers, but it is better to recite in a whisper if non-maḥram males can hear her voice.

Issue 192: It is obligatory to recite the four tasbīhs and Sūrat al-Fātiḥah silently in the third and fourth units of prayer, and based on obligatory precaution, one who recites Sūrat al-Fātiḥah must recite its bismillāh [saying: "In the Name of God"] in a whisper as well.

Issue 193: The obligation of reciting aloud or in a whisper in the first and second units of obligatory prayers is limited to the recitation of Sūrat al-Fātiḥah and the other Sūrah, just as the obligation of reciting in a whisper in the third and fourth units is limited to reciting Sūrat al-Fātiḥah or the four tasbīhs. As for the other utterances during bowing, prostration, testifying [tashahhud], salutation [taslīm], and other such recitations in the five daily prayers, the accountable person can choose between reciting aloud or in a whisper.

Issue 194: There is no difference in the obligation of reciting aloud or in a whisper in the daily obligatory prayers between performing them on time or making up for missed prayers, even if the make-up prayer is precautionary.

Issue 195: Reciting aloud entails audibly manifesting the essence of the sound, while reciting in a whisper means not manifesting it, even if someone next to him can hear his voice.

Issue 196: While reciting Sūrat al-Fātiḥah and the other Sūrah, if one recites excessively aloud in such a way that exceeds the norm, such as shouting, his prayer becomes invalid.

Issue 197: If one intentionally recites in a whisper where reciting aloud is obligatory or recites aloud intentionally where reciting in a whisper is obligatory, his prayer becomes invalid. However, if he does so due to forgetfulness or ignorance of the ruling, then the prayer is valid. If one remembers while reciting Sūrat al-Fātiḥah, the other Sūrah, or the four tasbīhs, there is no obligation to repeat what he mistakenly recited aloud or in a whisper.

Issue 198: It is obligatory to pronounce the words in recitation in a manner that indicates actual recitation. Merely reciting them in the heart without pronouncing them audibly is not sufficient. The criterion for this is that the worshiper can hear what he is reciting if he does not suffer from hearing impairment and there is no noise around him.

Issue 199: If a mute or someone unable to speak prays by gesture, his prayer is valid.

Issue 200: A person must perform the prayer correctly and without mistakes. If someone cannot learn it properly, he should pray to the best of his ability, and it is the recommended precaution to perfect it.

Issue 201: If someone cannot recite Sūrat al-Fātiḥah, the other Sūrah, or the other parts of the prayer correctly but is capable of learning, if he has sufficient time, he must learn. If time is limited, it is an obligatory precaution for him to perfect it if possible.

Issue 202: The criterion for the validity of recitation is based on observing the Arabic vowel and vowel-less diacritics of the letters and pronouncing them from their articulation points in a manner recognized by Arabic speakers as representing that specific letter and not another. Observing tajwīd rules is not obligatory.

Issue 203: If one does not know [how to pronounce] a word from Sūrat al-Fātiḥah or the other Sūrah, or intentionally avoids reciting it, or deliberately mispronounces a letter instead of another, such as pronouncing "z" ["ز"] instead of "ḍ" ["ض"], or alters the grammatical vowel marks, or fails to pronounce elongation, his prayer is invalidated.

Issue 204: If someone makes a mistake in recitation or in the other utterances of prayer, such as pronouncing the word "yūlad" ["يُولَد": begotten] with a kasrah vowel diacritic [ـِ] on the "lam" ["ل"], if he is a culpable ignorant,[16] then it is an obligatory precaution to consider his prayer invalid. However, if he is an inculpable ignorant[17] and thinks that what he recites is correct then his prayer is valid.

Issue 205: If one intends to connect one verse with another in recitation, it is not obligatory to utter the end vowel of the first verse. For example, there is no problem in reciting "māliki yawmi al-ddīni" with the "n" ["ن"] being vowel-less [sākin (ْ) instead of kasrah (ِ)] when connecting it with "iyyākā naʿbudū wa iyyākā nastaʿīn," and this is known as "connecting with sākin." Similarly, the same applies in connecting words within the same verse, although it is recommended precaution not to connect with sākin in the latter case.

Issue 206: There is no problem pausing and separating between parts of a single verse if it does not harm the integrity of the sentence. For example, reciting "walā al-ḍāllīn" with a short pause after "ghayri al-maghḍūb ʿalayhim."

Issue 207: If one doubts the correctness of the recitation of a verse after starting another, he should not pay attention to his doubt. Similarly, if he doubts the correctness of a

[16] A culpable ignorant [jāhil muqaṣṣir] is someone who is aware of his ignorance and knows of it but is negligent in learning the rulings.

[17] An inculpable ignorant [jāhil qāṣir] is unaware of his ignorance or knows of his ignorance but cannot find a way out of it.

sentence after starting another sentence, such as doubting the correctness of reciting "iyyākā naʿbudū" while saying "wa iyyākā nastaʿīn," he should not pay attention to his doubt. However, there is no problem in repeating the recitation of words whose correctness he doubts as a precaution.

Issue 208: The body of the worshiper must remain steady during the recitation of Sūrat al-Fātiḥah, the other Sūrah, or the four tasbīhs. If he intends to move forward or backward slightly or to move his body slightly to the right or left, he must stop the remembrance he is engaged in reciting.

Issue 209: It is recommended to:

- say "Aʿūdhū billāhī mina al-shayṭān al-rajīm" ["I seek refuge in God from the accursed Shayṭān"] before Sūrat al-Fātiḥah in the first unit of prayer;
- recite the "Bismillāh" ["In the Name of God"] aloud in Sūrat al-Fātiḥah and the other Sūrah in the first two units of Ẓuhr and ʿAṣr prayers;
- recite Sūrat al-Fātiḥah and the other Sūrah with great care;
- pause at verse endings;
- not to connect one verse with another;

- contemplate the meanings of the verses of Sūrat al-Fātiḥah and the other Sūrah while reciting them;

- say "alḥamdulillāhī Rabb al-ʿālamīn" ["praise be to God, Lord of the Worlds"] after completing Sūrat al-Fātiḥah, whether praying individually or in a congregation, whether as an Imām or a follower;

- say "Kathālika Allāhu Rabbī" once, twice, or thrice after reciting Sūrat al-Ikhlāṣ;

- pause for a moment after reciting Sūrat al-Fātiḥah and the other Sūrah, then continue the prayer.

Issue 210: It is recommended to seek forgiveness after the four tasbīhs in the third and fourth units of prayer by saying, for example: "astaghfirullah Rabbī wa atūbu ilayhi" ["I seek forgiveness from God, my Lord, and I turn to Him in repentance"] or "allāhumma ighfir lī" ["O God, forgive me"].

Issue 211: It is detestable [makrūh] to leave out Sūrat al-Ikhlāṣ in all five of the daily obligatory prayers, as well as to repeat a single Sūrah in two units of a single prayer, except for Sūrat al-Ikhlāṣ.

Issue 212: It is recommended in all prayers to recite Sūrat al-Qadr in the first unit and Sūrat al-Ikhlāṣ in the second unit of prayer.

Bowing [Rukūʿ]

Issue 213: It is obligatory to bow in every unit of prayer after recitation, meaning to incline to a degree where placing the hands on the knees is possible, and it is sufficient if the fingertips reach the knees.

Issue 214: It is an obligatory precaution to place the hands on the knees during bowing.

Issue 215: Bowing is a pillar [rukn] of prayer; bowing more or fewer times than prescribed intentionally or inadvertently invalidates the prayer. Therefore, if one raises his head after reaching the body's complete state of bowing and stillness, then inclines again intending to bow, or forgets to bow and remembers it during the second prostration or after it, his prayer becomes invalid.

Issue 216: Adding bowing to follow the imām (according to conditions mentioned later regarding congregational prayer) does not harm the prayer's validity; likewise, adding bowing advertently in the recommended prayer does not harm its validity.

Issue 217: One must bend forward to bow with the intention of bowing; therefore, if one bends forward for another purpose, like picking something up, it cannot be counted as bowing, and he must return to a standing position and then bend again for bowing. Such an action is not a pillar addition to the prayer and does not harm the validity of the prayer.

Issue 218: If one cannot physically perform the bowing, he should, if possible, bend using a support. If he cannot do so, he should bend as much as possible for him. In either case, performing bowing from a sitting position is not permissible, even if he can bend while sitting to the degree of bowing. Suppose he cannot physically bend to bow from a standing position at all. In that case, he must bow while sitting, and it is more precautious for him to perform another prayer while standing using gestures to indicate bowing. If he cannot bow even from a sitting position, he must bow with a gesture of his head from a standing position. If he cannot even incline his head while sitting to indicate bowing, he should close his eyes to indicate bowing and open them to indicate rising from the bow.

Issue 219: It suffices, for the bowing to be valid from a sitting position, that one inclines until his face becomes level with his knees, and it is not obligatory to place the hands on the knees.

Issue 220: Bowing more or less from a seated position or indicating it intentionally or inadvertently invalidates the prayer.

Issue 221: Remembering God [dhikr] when bowing is obligatory. The obligatory remembrance in bowing is "subḥāna Rabbiyal ʿaẓīm wa biḥamdihi" ["glory is to my

Lord, the Most Great, and praise is due to Him"] once, or "subḥānallāh" ["glory be to God"] three times. Also, other remembrances such as "alḥamdulillāh" ["praise be to God"] and "Allāhu Akbar" ["God is the Greatest"] (except for the remembrance specific to prostration) suffice in the same amount.

Issue 222: In cases of necessity and time constraint, it suffices to say "subḥānallāh" once.

Issue 223: During the obligatory remembrance in bowing, it is also obligatory that the body be steady and tranquil. It is an obligatory precaution to maintain the stillness of the body even during the remembrances recited with the intention of recommendation [mustaḥabb] during bowing, such as repeating the obligatory remembrance [tasbīḥah al-kubra] and similar remembrances.

Issue 224: If one intends to move slightly forward or backward or move his body slightly to the right or left, he must cease the remembrance he is engaged in. However, there is no problem in reciting remembrances performed with the intention of general remembrance, not specifically for prayer, during movement.

Issue 225: There is no harm in slight bodily movement or movement of the fingers and the like while reciting remembrance in bowing.

Issue 226: If the body moves during the obligatory remembrance involuntarily, causing it to deviate from the required steadiness, the remembrance must be repeated after the re-establishment of steadiness.

Issue 227: Whoever knows the obligation of tranquility during the obligatory remembrance for bowing, if he begins it deliberately before reaching the full bowing position and achieving tranquility of his body, his prayer becomes invalid.

Issue 228: If he starts with the remembrance inadvertently before reaching the full bowing position and bodily tranquility, he must repeat it after reaching the full bowing position.

Issue 229: Whoever knows the obligation of tranquility during the bowing remembrance and rises from bowing deliberately before completing the remembrance, his prayer becomes invalid. However, if he does so inadvertently, he realizes that before rising from the full bowing position, he must remain in that position tranquility and recite the bowing remembrance. If he realizes that after rising from the full bowing position, his prayer is valid.

Issue 230: If someone is unable—due to illness or the like—to remain in the bowing position long enough for him to recite the remembrance "subḥānallāh" three times, once is sufficient. If he can only remain for one moment, it is an obligatory precaution to start reciting the remembrance at that moment and complete it upon rising.

Issue 231: After completing the bowing remembrance, it is obligatory to raise the head until fully erect and tranquil and proceed to prostration. If someone prostrates deliberately before rising or attaining tranquility, his prayer is invalid.

Issue 232: If one forgets to bow and remembers before reaching prostration, he should return to standing and bow from the standing position. It is not sufficient for him to go into bowing while in a bent position; if he does so, his prayer becomes invalid.

Issue 233: If one forgets the bowing and remembers after entering the first prostration or after raising his head from it, but before entering the second prostration, he should return to standing, then bow, then perform the two prostrations and complete his prayer. It is recommended that precautions be taken to perform the two prostrations of forgetfulness after the prayer for the additional prostration.

Issue 234: It is recommended [mustaḥabb] before bowing to say takbīr while standing upright. It is also recommended for a man to push his knees back, not incline his head, stretch his neck forth keeping it in line with his back, place his hands on his knees, look between his feet, send blessings upon the Prophet and his family before or after the remembrance, repeat the bowing remembrance, conclude it on an odd count, and say "samiʿal lāhu liman ḥamidah" ["God hears the one who praises Him"] after standing up erect and tranquil.

Issue 235: It is recommended that women place their hands above their knees and not push their knees back.

Prostration

Issue 236: After bowing in every unit of the obligatory and recommended prayers, two prostrations are obligatory, meaning placing the forehead on the ground in submission to God ﷻ.

Issue 237: It is obligatory in prostration to place the forehead, the inner parts of the palms, the knees, and the tips of the big toes on the ground.

Issue 238: Performing both prostrations together in one unit of prayer is a pillar of prayer. Hence, the prayer becomes invalid if they are omitted intentionally or inadvertently or if two additional prostrations are added intentionally or inadvertently in one unit of prayer.

Issue 239: Intentionally adding or omitting one prostration invalidates the prayer.

Issue 240: The prayer is not invalidated by adding or omitting one prostration inadvertently or due to forgetfulness, but it has specific rulings, which will be explained later.

Issue 241: If one does not place the forehead on the ground intentionally or inadvertently, the prostration is not fulfilled even if the other six body parts (inner parts of the palms, knees, and tips of the big toes) are placed on the ground. However, if the forehead is placed on the ground but the other body parts are not placed on it inadvertently, or if the remembrance is not uttered inadvertently, then the prayer remains valid.

Issue 242: It is permissible during prostration to place the rest of the toes on the ground along the tips of the two big toes.

Issue 243: The obligatory remembrance during prostration is "subḥāna Rabbiyal aʿlā wa biḥamdihi" ["glory is to my Lord, the Most High, and praise is due to Him"] once, or "subḥānallāh" ["glory be to God"] three time. Other remembrances such as "Alhamdulillah" and "Allāhu Akbar" (except for the remembrance specific to bowing) are also sufficient in the same quantity. Also, other remembrances such as "alḥamdulillāh" ["praise be to God"] and "Allāhu Akbar" ["God is the Greatest"] and the like (except for the remembrance specific to bowing) suffice in the same amount.

Issue 244: If one utters the remembrance of bowing instead of the remembrance of prostration, or vice versa, if it was done inadvertently, there is no issue. Similarly, the same applies if it was done intentionally with the intention of general remembrance of God ﷻ, but one must also utter the specific remembrance.

Issue 245: If one realizes after bowing or prostration that he made a mistake in remembrance, his prayer remains valid.

Issue 246: It is obligatory to have tranquility during the obligatory remembrance in prostration, and it is preferable to maintain tranquility during the remembrance performed with the intention of recommendation [mustaḥabb] in prostration, such as repeating "subḥāna Rabbiyal a'lā wa biḥamdihi" and the like.

Issue 247: If one knows the necessity of tranquility during the obligatory remembrance in prostration if he intentionally starts reciting the remembrance before the forehead touches the ground and before achieving tranquility, his prayer becomes invalid. Similarly, the same applies if one intentionally raises his head from prostration before completing the remembrance.

Issue 248: If one utters the remembrance of prostration inadvertently before the forehead touches the ground and before achieving tranquility, he must repeat it after achieving tranquility.

Issue 249: If one realizes after raising his head from prostration that he uttered the remembrance before reaching the prostration, achieving tranquility, or raising his head from prostration before completing the remembrance, his prayer remains valid.

Issue 250: If one prostrates on a mattress or the like (things on which the body moves first before settling and achieving tranquility), if he utters the remembrance when the body is settled, his prayer is valid.

Issue 251: If one intentionally raises any of the seven points of prostration from the ground during the remembrance, his prayer becomes invalid. However, if one raises any of these points, except for the forehead, without being engaged in the remembrance, there is no issue.

Issue 252: If one inadvertently raises his forehead from the ground before completing the remembrance of prostration, he cannot return it to the ground again, and it counts as one prostration. However, if one inadvertently raises the other parts of his body from the ground, he must place them back and utter the remembrance.

Issue 253: If the forehead collides with the place of prostration and is forcibly lifted from the ground, one must place his forehead back on the ground, uttering the remembrance of prostration again, and all this counts as one prostration.

Issue 254: It is obligatory to voluntarily place the palms on the ground during prostration. However, placing the back of the hands is permissible if necessary. If unable to do so, one may place the wrists. If he can also not do so, any part that can be placed on the ground up to the elbow is acceptable. If that is not possible, placing the forearm is permissible.

Issue 255: After completing the remembrance of the first prostration, it is obligatory to raise the head from it and sit calmly, then bend down for the second prostration.

Issue 256: If someone—due to illness or the like—cannot remain in the prostration position long enough to utter the remembrance "subḥānallāh" three times, then once is sufficient. Suppose he can only stay in the prostration position for just one moment. In that case, it is an obligatory precaution that he starts uttering the remembrance at that moment and completes it when rising.

Issue 257: If someone cannot bring his forehead to the ground, he should bow as much as they can and place the turbah—or any other thing permitted to prostrate—on an elevated object. He should then place his forehead on it in a manner that passes for a valid prostration. He must also place his palms, knees, and the tips of his big toes on the ground in the customary manner if possible. If he cannot find anything to place the turbah on, he should lift it with his hands and place his forehead on it. He should nod his head instead of prostrating if he cannot bend down at all. If that is not possible, then he should indicate with his eyes.

Issue 258: During prostration, the position of the forehead must not be higher or lower than the position of the knees and the tips of the toes by more than the width of four closed fingers.

Issue 259: The turbah, or any other thing it is permitted to prostrate, must be pure. However, there is no issue in placing the turbah on an impure carpet if the impurity does not reach the body or clothes. There is also no problem with one side of the soil being impure, provided the praying person places his forehead on the clean side.

Issue 260: There must be no barrier between the praying person's forehead and what he prostrates upon, such as hair, turban, etc.

Issue 261: If there were a barrier between the forehead and the turbah, the prayer would become invalid. However, if only the color of the turbah changes, there is no problem with that.

Issue 262: If, while in prostration, one notices a barrier preventing his forehead from touching the turbah, such as a cloak and the like, he must, without lifting his head from the turbah, adjust his forehead away from the obstacle or move the turbah under his forehead until his forehead meets the turbah by at least the length of the fingertips. If one raises his head from the turbah, removes the obstacle, and then places his forehead back down, if this action is done out of ignorance or forgetfulness, the prayer remains valid for one prostration in one unit of prayer. However, if done knowingly or intentionally, or if performed in two prostrations of a single unit of prayer, the prayer becomes invalid.

Issue 263: Based on obligatory precaution, in the first unit of every prayer and the third unit of four-unit prayers, one must sit briefly after the second prostration and then rise for the next unit. However, if one rises directly to the next unit without sitting briefly, his prayer does not become invalid.

Things On Which Prostration Is Permitted

Issue 264: The forehead must be placed on something upon which prostration is valid.

Issue 265: The place that the forehead touches in prostration during prayer must be from the earth or from what the earth produces, excluding what is edible or worn, such as stone, dirt, wood, tree leaves, etc. It is not permissible to prostrate on what is edible or worn, even if it is produced by the earth, such as wheat and cotton, nor on things that are not considered parts of the earth [anymore], such as metals, glass, and the like.

Issue 266: It is permissible to prostrate on marble stones and other stones used in the construction or decoration of houses, as well as on agate, turquoise, pearls, and the like. However, it is recommended precaution not to prostrate on the latter group.[18]

Issue 267: It is permissible to prostrate on baked clay [e.g., bricks], baked lime, gypsum, concrete, and cement.

Issue 268: It is permissible to prostrate on plants that grow from the earth and are used only as animal feed, such as straw and grass.

Issue 269: It is not permissible, based on precaution, to prostrate on green tea leaves. However, prostration is permissible on coffee leaves not used for consumption.

Issue 270: It is permissible to prostrate on non-edible flowers and medicinal herbs that grow from the earth and are used only for treating diseases, such as hibiscus and lavender flowers. As for herbs used for purposes other than treatment, they are also eaten because of their medicinal properties, such as khabbah and the like, so it is not permissible to prostrate them.

Issue 271: Plants considered edible in some regions or by some people, but others not used for food consumption are considered edible, and their prostration is invalid.

---

[18] Agate, turquoise, and pearls.

Issue 272: It is permissible to prostrate on papers made from wood and plants (excluding cotton and flax).

Issue 273: If one cannot find something on which prostration is permitted or cannot prostrate on it due to cold or heat or the like if his clothing is made of cotton or flax, or if he has something else made of cotton or flax, he may prostrate on it instead. Based on obligatory precaution, when cotton or flax is available, one must not prostrate on anything else (i.e., other than that type of garment). If nothing of the sort is available, it is an obligatory precaution to prostrate on the back of one's hand.

Issue 274: If one loses what he used to prostrate during prayer and nothing valid for prostration is within his reach, if there is enough time, he must break his prayer. If time is limited, he should follow the order mentioned in the previous issue.

Issue 275: It is permissible to prostrate on carpets and the like in situations where taqiyyah[19] is obligatory, and there is no obligation to go elsewhere. However, if prostration can be done in that place on hay or rocks, it is an obligatory precaution to choose them.

Issue 276: If the turbah sticks to the forehead in the first prostration, it must be removed before the second. If it is

---

[19] Taqiyyah means precautionary dissimulation or denial of religious 68 belief and practice in the face of persecution.

not removed and prostration is done in that state, the validity of the prayer is subject to doubt.

Issue 277: The best prostration is on soil and the earth, as it signifies submission and humility before God, and no turbah for prostration equals the turbah of the Master of Martyrs ؑ [i.e., the turbah made from the soil around his holy grave].

Issue 278: Recommended acts of prostration are as follows:

1. Saying "Allāhu Akbar" ["God is the Greatest"] before and after prostration when the body is settled.

2. Saying between the two prostrations: "Astaghfirullah Rabbī wa atūbu ilayhi" ["I seek forgiveness from God, my Lord, and I turn to Him in repentance"].

3. Prolonging the prostration, remembering God, supplicating for worldly and Hereafter needs, and sending blessings upon the Prophet and his family.

4. Repeating remembrance of God and concluding with an odd number of remembrances.

5. Sitting after prostration by placing weight on the left thigh and the top part of the right foot on the sole of his left foot.

6. Saying while rising for the next standing position: "Bi-ḥawli Allāhi wa quwwatihi aqūmu wa aqʿudu" ["By God's power and might, I rise and I sit"].

Issue 279. It is detestable [makrūh] to recite the Qur'ān during prostration.

Issue 280: Prostration to anyone other than God is forbidden. As for the people who place their foreheads on the ground in front of the Imāms' ﷺ shrines, if done with the intention of thanking God ﷻ, it is permissible; otherwise, it is not permissible.

Prostration of Recitation

Issue 281: In each of the following four chapters: Sūrat as-Sajdah, Sūrat Fuṣṣilat, Sūrat an-Najm, and Sūrat al-ʿAlaq, there is a verse that, if a person reads or listens to it, he must prostrate immediately after finishing it. If he delays it due to forgetfulness, he must perform it upon remembering.[20]

Issue 282: The reason for the obligation of prostration is the entire verse, so prostration is not obligatory by reading or listening to only some part of the verse.

---

[20] The verses that contain the obligatory prostration of recitation are:

a. Verse 15, Chapter 32 (Sūrat al-Sajdah);
b. Verse 37, Chapter 41 (Sūrat Fuṣṣilat);
c. Verse 62, Chapter 53 (Sūrat al-Najm);
d. and Verse 19, Chapter 96, (Sūrat al-ʿAlaq).

Issue 283: Prostration is not obligatory by reading or listening to the translation of the mentioned verses.

Issue 284: Prostration is obligatory if one listens to the verse of prostration broadcasted on the radio, television, recording devices, and the like.

Issue 285: If someone reads the verse of obligatory prostration and another person or a recording device and the like simultaneously listens to it, prostration becomes obligatory twice.

Issue 286: In the prostration of recitation, one must prostrate something upon which prostration is valid in prayer. Other conditions for prostration in prayer, such as facing the Qiblah and being in a state of ablution, are not obligatory to observe for a prostration of recitation.

Issue 287: Simply placing the forehead on the ground is sufficient for the prostration of recitation, and uttering remembrance of God is not obligatory, although it is recommended. It is preferable to say:

"Lā ilāha illal lāhu ḥaqqan ḥaqqa, lā ilāha illal lāhu iymānan wa taṣdīqa, lā ilāha illal lāhu ʿubūdiyyatan wa riqqa, sajadtu laka yā rabbi taʿabbudan wa riqqa, lā mustankifan wa lā mustakbīra, bal anā ʿabdun dhalīlun ḍaʿīfun khāʾifun mustajīr."

Translation: "There is no god but God, truly, truly. There is no god but God. I believe in this certainly, and I affirm it certainly. There is no god but God; I testify this in servitude and as a slave. I prostrate to You, O my Lord, in servitude and as a slave, not disdainfully nor arrogantly. Rather, I am a servant lowly, weak, fearing, and seeking refuge."

Testifying [Tashahhud]

Issue 288: After the second prostration of the second and last units of prayer in all prayers, the worshiper must sit and recite—after settling down and achieving a state of tranquility—several phrases that serve as testification, and this act is called "tashahhud."

Issue 289: The obligatory recitation in the tashahhud is:

"Ashhadu an lā ilāha illal lāhu waḥdahu lā sharīka lah, wa ashhadu anna muḥammadan ʿabduhu wa rasūluh, allāhumma ṣalli ʿalā muḥammadin wa āli muḥammad."

Translation: "I testify that there is no god but God, He alone, for whom there is no partner. And I testify that Muḥammad is His servant and His messenger. O God! Bless Muḥammad and the progeny of Muḥammad."

Issue 290: It is recommended before the obligatory recitation in the tashahhud to say: "alḥamdulillāh ["praise be to God"] or "bismillāhi wa billāh, wal ḥamdu lillāh, wa khayrul asmāʾi lillāh" ["in the name of God, and by God, and all praise is for God, and the best names belong to God"]. It is also recommended after sending blessings upon the Prophet and his family to say: "wa taqabbal shafāʿatahu warfaʿ darajatah" ["and accept his [i.e. the Prophet's] intercession and raise his rank"].

Issue 291: The tashahhud is a non-pillar obligatory act of prayer. Deliberately adding to or subtracting from it invalidates the prayer, while doing so inadvertently does not invalidate it.

Issue 292: If one forgets to recite the tashahhud and stands for the third unit of prayer but remembers before bowing, he should sit and recite the tashahhud, then stand and recite the four tasbīḥs of the third unit again and complete his prayer. It is recommended precaution to perform the two prostrations of forgetfulness after the prayer for the extra standing.

Issue 293: If one forgets to recite the tashahhud and remembers during the bowing of the third unit of prayer or after it, he should complete his prayer and perform the two prostrations of forgetfulness after the prayer. Based on obligatory precaution, one must make up for the missed tashahhud before them.

Salutation [Taslīm]

Issue 294: Salutation is the final part of the prayer, and the prayer is concluded by uttering it. The obligatory taslīm is to say: "Assalāmu ʿalaykum" [Peace be upon you]. And it is preferable to add: "wa raḥmatul lāhi wa barakātuh" [and God's mercy and His blessings (be upon you too)], or to say: "Assalāmu ʿalaynā wa ʿalā ʿibādil lāhiṣ ṣāliḥīn" [Peace be upon us and the righteous servants of God].

Issue 295: It is recommended to say before the preceding two taslīms: "Assalāmu ʿalayka ayyuhan nabiyyu wa raḥmatul lāhi wa barakātuh" [Peace be upon you O Prophet, and God's mercy and His blessings (be upon you too)].

Issue 296: Salutation is a non-pillar obligatory act of prayer, so the prayer is not invalidated by adding to it or omitting it advertently.

Issue 297: If one forgets the salutation and remembers before the form of the prayer is broken up and he has not done something that intentionally or inadvertently invalidates it, such as turning his back to the Qiblah, he should recite the taslīms, and his prayer remains valid.

Sequence [Tartīb]

Issue 298: It is obligatory for the praying person to perform the acts of prayer in the prescribed sequence and to perform each part of it in its designated place. Therefore, if one deliberately disregards the prescribed sequence, such as reciting a Sūrah before Sūrat al-Fātiḥah or performing prostration before bowing, his prayer becomes invalid.

Issue 299: If one forgets a pillar of the prayer and remembers after starting the next pillar, such as forgetting the two prostrations (pillar) and remembering after starting the bowing (pillar) of the next unit of prayer, his prayer becomes invalid.

Issue 300: If one forgets a pillar and remembers after starting the non-pillar part that follows it, such as forgetting the prostration and remembering after starting the tashahhud, he must return to perform the pillar and then repeat the non-pillar part he inadvertently skipped. For example, suppose the praying person remembers that after starting with tashahhud (non-pillar), he did not perform the two prostrations (pillar). In that case, he must recite tashahhud again after performing the prostrations.

Issue 301: If one forgets a non-pillar part and remembers after starting the pillar act that follows it, such as forgetting to recite Sūrat al-Fātiḥah (non-pillar) and remembering after starting the bowing (pillar), his prayer remains valid, and it is not permissible for him to return to the standing position to perform it.

Issue 302: If one forgets a non-pillar part and performs the non-pillar part that follows it and remembers before starting a subsequent pillar act, such as forgetting Sūrat al-Fātiḥah (non-pillar) and reciting the other Sūrah (non-pillar), then remembering before starting the bowing (pillar), he must perform the part he forgot (Sūrat al-Fātiḥah) and then repeat the part he recited (the other Sūrah).

Close Succession [Muwālāt]

Issue 303: The worshiper must observe successiveness between the parts of the prayer, such as bowing, prostration, tashahhud, and the like, without leaving long and uncustomary time intervals between them. This is referred to as "close succession" [muwālāt]. Accordingly, if the time gap between the parts of the prayer reaches a point that the observer considers breaking up the form of the prayer, the prayer becomes invalid.

Issue 304: If one inadvertently makes a prolonged pause between words or within a single word beyond the customary limit, but it does not reach the point of nullifying the structure of the prayer, and he realizes that after starting with the next pillar act, then his prayer remains valid, and there is no obligation to repeat those words or sentences. However, if he realizes that before starting with the next pillar, he must return and repeat [the sentence or word].

Issue 305: Prolonging the bowing and prostration and reciting lengthy chapters of the Qur'ān do not nullify the close succession.

Qunūt

Issue 306: It is recommended [mustaḥabb] to raise the hands and supplicate after reciting Sūrat al-Fātiḥah and the other Sūrah and before bowing in the second unit of all obligatory and recommended prayers, and this is what is known as "Qunūt."

Issue 307: In the Friday prayer, there is Qunūt in each unit, with Qunūt in the first unit before bowing and Qunūt in the second unit after bowing.

Issue 308: In the 'Īd (Eid) prayers, both 'Īd al-Fiṭr and 'Īd al-Aḍḥa, there are five Qunūts in the first unit and four Qunūts in the second unit.

Issue 309: It is permissible during Qunūt to recite any remembrance, supplication, or verse from the Qur'ān. It is also permissible to limit it to sending blessings upon the Prophet and his family once or saying "subḥānallāh" [glory be to God], "bismillāh" [in the name of God], or "bismillāh al-raḥmān al-raḥīm" [in the name of God, the Beneficent, the Merciful]. However, it is better to recite supplications mentioned in the Qur'ān, such as:

"Rabbana ātinā fī d-dunyā ḥasanatan wa fī-l-ākhirati ḥasanatan waqinā ʿadhāban-nār."

Translation: "Our Lord, give us in this world [that which is] good and in the Hereafter [that which is] good and protect us from the punishment of the Fire."

Or, supplications and remembrances narrated from the Infallibles عليهم السلام, such as:

"Lā ilāha illal lāhul ḥalīmul karīm, lā ilāha illal lāhul ʿaliyyul ʿaẓīm, subḥānal lāhi rabbis samāwātis sabʿ, wa rabbil araḍīnas sabʿ, wa mā fīhinna wa mā baynahunna wa rabbil ʿarshil ʿaẓīm, wal ḥamdu lillāhi rabbil ʿālamīn."

Translation: "There is no god but God, the Forbearing, the Generous. There is no god but God, the High, the Great. I declare emphatically that God is free from imperfections, [God,] Lord of the seven skies, all that is in them, and all that is between them, and Lord of the Great Throne. And all praise is for God, Lord of the Worlds."

Issue 310: Supplicating, seeking forgiveness, and asking for needs in Persian or any other language is permissible.

Issue 311: It is recommended to recite Qunūt aloud. However, it is not recommended in congregational prayers if the Imām can hear the follower's voice [i.e., the person praying in the congregation prayer following the lead of the Imām].

Supplications After Prayer [Taʿqībāt]

Issue 312: It is recommended for the praying person, after completing the prayer, to engage in supplication, remembrance of God, and Qurʾān recitation. These actions are referred to as "taʿqībāt." It is preferable in this case for the individual to sit facing the Qiblah and to be in a state of ablution or purification or have performed dry ablution [tayammum].

Issue 313: The taʿqībāt does not need to be uttered in Arabic, but it is preferable to recite the supplications and remembrances narrated from the Infallibles عليهم السلام. Among the most virtuous of these is the remembrance known as "Tasbīh al-Zahrāʾ عليها السلام," which consists of thirty-four times "Allāhu akbar" [God is the Greatest], thirty-three times "alḥamdulillāh" [praise be to God], and thirty-three times "subḥānallāh" [glory be to God]. In books of supplications, there are taʿqībāt with sublime contents and beautiful expressions attributed to the Infallibles عليهم السلام.

Issue 314: It is recommended to perform the prostration of thanksgiving [sajdat al-shukr] after the prayer by placing one's forehead on the ground in gratitude for all blessings and the blessing of success in performing the prayer. It is preferable to say three times or more: "Shukran Allāh" [thanks to God].

Issue 315: It is recommended for the praying person to recite the words of the prayer and its remembrances with focus, humility, and presence of heart, seizing the opportunity of prayer to purify the soul and draw closer to God, the Exalted.

Translation of the Prayer

Issue 316: Sūrat al-Fātiḥah:

﴿بِسۡمِ ٱللَّهِ ٱلرَّحۡمَٰنِ ٱلرَّحِيمِ﴾

﴾*bi-smi llāhi r-raḥmāni r-raḥīm*^{i}﴿

﴿ٱلۡحَمۡدُ لِلَّهِ رَبِّ ٱلۡعَٰلَمِينَ﴾

﴾^{a}*l-ḥamdu li-llāhi rabbi l-ʿālamīn*^{a}﴿

﴿ٱلرَّحۡمَٰنِ ٱلرَّحِيمِ﴾

﴾^{a}*r-raḥmāni r-raḥīm*^{i}﴿

﴿مَٰلِكِ يَوۡمِ ٱلدِّينِ﴾

﴾*māliki yawmi d-dīn*^{i}﴿

﴿إِيَّاكَ نَعۡبُدُ وَإِيَّاكَ نَسۡتَعِينُ﴾

﴾*ʾiyyāka naʿbudu wa-ʾiyyāka nastaʿīn*^{u}﴿

﴿ٱهْدِنَا ٱلصِّرَٰطَ ٱلْمُسْتَقِيمَ﴾

﴾*[i]hdinā ṣ-ṣirāṭa l-mustaqīm[a]*﴿

﴿صِرَٰطَ ٱلَّذِينَ أَنْعَمْتَ عَلَيْهِمْ غَيْرِ ٱلْمَغْضُوبِ عَلَيْهِمْ وَلَا ٱلضَّآلِّينَ﴾

﴾*ṣirāṭa lladhīna 'an'amta 'alayhim ghayri l-maghḍūbi 'alayhim wa-lā ḍ-ḍāllīn[a]*﴿

﴾*In the Name of God, the Beneficent, the Merciful. All praise belongs to God, Lord of all the worlds, the Beneficent, the Merciful, Master of the Day of Retribution. You [alone] do we worship, and to You [alone] do we turn for help. Guide us on the straight path, the path of those whom You have blessed — such as have not incurred Your wrath, nor are astray*﴿

Issue 317: Sūrat al-Ikhlāṣ:

﴿قُلْ هُوَ ٱللَّهُ أَحَدٌ﴾

﴾*qul huwa llāhu 'aḥad[un-i]*﴿

﴿ٱللَّهُ ٱلصَّمَدُ﴾

﴾*[a]llāhu ṣ-ṣamad[u]*﴿

﴿لَمْ يَلِدْ وَلَمْ يُولَدْ﴾

﴿lam yalid wa-lam yūlad﴾

﴿وَلَمْ يَكُن لَّهُۥ كُفُوًا أَحَدُۢ﴾

﴿wa-lam yakun lahū kufuwan 'aḥad[un]*﴾*

﴿Say, 'He is God, the One. God is the Embracing. He neither begat, nor was begotten, nor has He any equal.'﴾

Issue 318: Translations of the dhikr of rukūʿ and sajdah and some mustaḥabb phrases are as follows:

سُبْحَانَ اللَّهِ

Subḥāna Allāh

Glory be to God

سُبْحَانَ رَبِّيَ العَظِيمِ وَبِحَمْدِهِ

Subḥāna Rabbīya al-ʿAẓīmi wa-bi-ḥamdih

Glory be to my Lord, the Magnificent, and with His praise

سُبْحَانَ رَبِّيَ الْأَعْلَى وَبِحَمْدِهِ

Subḥāna Rabbīya al-Aʿlā wa-bi-ḥamdih

Glory be to my Lord, the Most High, and with His praise

سَمِعَ اللَّهُ لِمَنْ حَمِدَهُ

Samiʿa Allāhu li-man ḥamidah

God hears the one who praises Him

أَسْتَغْفِرُ اللَّهَ رَبِّيَ وَأَتُوبُ إِلَيْهِ

Astaghfiru Allāha Rabbīya wa-atūbu ilayh

I seek forgiveness from God, my Lord, and I turn to Him in repentance

بِحَوْلِ اللَّهِ وَقُوَّتِهِ أَقُومُ وَأَقْعُدُ

Bi-ḥawli Allāhi wa-quwwatihī aqūmu wa-aqʿud

By the might and power of God, I stand and I sit

Issue 319: Translation of the dhikr of qunūt are as follows:

رَبَّنَا آتِنَا فِي الدُّنْيَا حَسَنَةً وَفِي الآخِرَةِ حَسَنَةً وَقِنَا عَذَابَ النَّارِ

Rabbana ātinā fī al-dunyā ḥasanatan wa-fī al-ākhirati ḥasanatan wa-qinā ʿadhāba al-nār

Our Lord, grant us goodness in this world and goodness in the Hereafter, and protect us from the punishment of the Fire.

لَا إِلٰهَ إِلَّا اللّٰهُ الْحَلِيمُ الْكَرِيمُ

Lā ilāha illā Allāhu al-ḥalīmu al-karīm

There is no god except God, the Forbearing, the Generous.

لَا إِلٰهَ إِلَّا اللّٰهُ الْعَلِيُّ الْعَظِيمُ

Lā ilāha illā Allāhu al-ʿAliyyu al-ʿAẓīm

There is no god except God, the Most High, the Magnificent.

سُبْحَانَ اللّٰهِ رَبِّ السَّمَاوَاتِ السَّبْعِ

Subḥāna Allāhi Rabbi al-samāwāti al-sabʿ

Glory be to God, the Lord of the seven heavens.

وَرَبِّ الْأَرَضِينَ السَّبْعِ

Wa-Rabbi al-arāḍīna al-sab'

And the Lord of the seven earths.

وَمَا فِيهِنَّ وَمَا بَيْنَهُنَّ

Wa-mā fihinna wa-mā baynahunna

And whatever is in them and whatever is between them.

وَرَبِّ الْعَرْشِ الْعَظِيمِ

Wa-Rabbi al-'Arshi al-'Aẓīm

And the Lord of the Mighty Throne.

وَالْحَمْدُ لِلَّهِ رَبِّ الْعَالَمِينَ

Wa-al-ḥamdu li-llāhi Rabbi al-'ālamīn

And all praise is due to God, the Lord of all worlds.

Issue 320: The translation of the four tasbīḥ is as follows:

سُبْحانَ اللهِ

Subḥāna Allāh

Glory be to God

وَالحَمْدُ لِلهِ

Wa-al-ḥamdu li-llāh

and all praise is due to God

وَ لاَ اِلَهَ اِلاَّ اللهُ

Wa-lā ilāha illā Allāh

and there is no god except God

وَ اللهُ اَكْبَرُ

Wa-Allāhu akbar

and God is the Greatest

Issue 321: The translation of tashahhud and salām is as follows:

اَلْحَمْدُ لِلَّهِ

Al-ḥamdu li-llāh

All praise is due to God.

اَشْهَدُ اَنْ لَا إِلٰهَ إِلَّا اللَّهُ

Ashhadu an lā ilāha illā Allāh

I bear witness that there is no god except God.

وَحْدَهُ لَا شَرِيكَ لَهُ

Waḥdahu lā sharīka lah

He is One, there is no partner with Him.

وَأَشْهَدُ أَنَّ مُحَمَّدًا عَبْدُهُ وَرَسُولُهُ

Wa-ashhadu anna Muḥammadan ʿabduhū wa-rasūluh

And I bear witness that Muḥammad is His servant and messenger.

اَللّٰهُمَّ صَلِّ عَلَىٰ مُحَمَّدٍ وَآلِ مُحَمَّدٍ

Allāhumma ṣalli ʿalā Muḥammadin wa-āli Muḥammad

O God, send blessings upon Muḥammad and the family of Muḥammad.

وَتَقَبَّلْ شَفَاعَتَهُ وَارْفَعْ دَرَجَتَهُ

Wa-taqabbal shafāʿatahū wa-rfaʿ darajatah

And accept his intercession and elevate his rank.

اَلسَّلَامُ عَلَيْنَا وَعَلَىٰ عِبَادِ اللّٰهِ الصَّالِحِينَ

Al-salāmu ʿalaynā wa-ʿalā ʿibādi Allāhi al-ṣāliḥīn

Peace be upon us and upon the righteous servants of God.

اَلسَّلَامُ عَلَيْكُمْ وَرَحْمَةُ اللّٰهِ وَبَرَكَاتُهُ

Al-salāmu ʿalaykum wa-raḥmatu Allāhi wa-barakātuh

Peace be upon you, and the mercy of God, and His blessings.

Things That Invalidate [Mubṭilāt] Prayer

Issue 322: Things that invalidate prayer are as follows:

1. The absence of any conditions that must be observed in prayer.
2. Invalidity of the partial-body ablution [wuḍūʾ] or major ablution [ghusl].
3. Deviation from the Qiblah direction.
4. Speaking.
5. Laughing.
6. Crying.
7. Breaking up the form of prayer.
8. Eating and drinking.
9. Doubts that invalidate the prayer.[21]
10. Adding or omitting the pillars of the prayer.
11. Saying "Amīn" after reciting Sūrat al-Fātiḥah.
12. Placing one hand over the other in front of the body (crossing them).

---

[21] These will be explained in the section on doubts.

Issue 323: If one of the conditions that must be observed during prayer is not met, such as if one realizes during prayer that the place is invaded, the prayer becomes invalid.

Issue 324: If something occurs during prayer that invalidates wuḍū', ghusl, or tayammum [dry ablution], such as if one falls asleep during prayer or urinates during it, the prayer becomes invalid.

Issue 325: If one intentionally turns his face or body away from the Qiblah direction to see his right or left side easily, his prayer becomes invalid. If he does this inadvertently, it is an obligatory precaution that his prayer also becomes invalid. However, a slight face turning towards either side does not invalidate the prayer.

Issue 326: If one intentionally speaks during prayer, even a single word, his prayer becomes invalid.

Issue 327: Sounds produced when coughing, sneezing, or clearing his throat do not invalidate the prayer, even if they produce a sound.

Issue 328: If someone says a word intending it as a remembrance of God, such as "Allāhu Akbar" [God is the Greatest], and raises his voice while uttering it to make someone aware of something, there is no problem. However, if he does not make an intention of remembrance at all, or he makes an intention for both purposes [i.e., intention to utter remembrance and intention to make someone aware of something], then his prayer becomes invalid.

Issue 329: It is not permissible for the praying person to initiate saying salām [the Islāmic greeting] to others. However, if someone greets him, it is obligatory to return the greeting. His response should begin with the word "salām," as if saying "salāmun ʿalaykum" or "as-salāmu ʿalaykum" back. It is not permissible to say "ʿalaykum as-salām" back [which is the typical response outside prayer].

Issue 330: If someone greets a group of people saying, "As-salāmu ʿalaykum to all of you," and one of them is praying, then if another person responds to him, it is not permissible for the one praying to respond.

Issue 331: It is obligatory to respond to the greeting of peace from a mumayyiz child—i.e., a child who can discern right and wrong—as it is for adults.

Issue 332: Responding to the greeting of peace is an immediate obligation. If delaying the response for any reason makes it unbelievable to respond to that greeting, responding is not permissible if it is during prayer. However, if it is outside of prayer, it is not obligatory. The same ruling applies regarding doubt about reaching the level of delay mentioned. If deliberately delaying the response to the greeting, it constitutes disobedience.

Issue 333: When greeting a praying person, if the word "salām" is used instead of "as-salāmu ʿalaykum" and if it is understood as the customary greeting of peace, the response is obligatory, and as a precaution, the response should be given in the same manner as described previously.

Issue 334: Deliberate laughter with sound (aloud) invalidates the prayer, while inadvertent laughter or laughter without sound does not invalidate it.

Issue 335: If the praying person cannot control his laughter and his abdomen fills with laughter, causing his face to turn red or his body to shake, his prayer remains valid unless it disrupts the form of the prayer.

Issue 336: Deliberate crying with sound (aloud) for worldly matters invalidates the prayer, but if it stems from fear of God and matters of the Hereafter, then it is permissible and even a most commendable act.

Issue 337: Any action that disrupts the form of the prayer, such as clapping or jumping in the air, invalidates the prayer, intentionally or inadvertently.

Issue 338: Gesturing with one's hand, eye, or eyebrow to convey a message to someone or respond to their question, if it does not disrupt the tranquility and composure or break up the form of the prayer, does not harm its validity.

Issue 339: Closing one's eyes during prayer is not problematic and does not invalidate it, although it is detestable [makrūḥ] outside of bowing.

Issue 340: Passing the hands over the face after the Qunūt is detestable but does not invalidate the prayer.

Issue 341: Eating and drinking during the prayer invalidate it, whether a little or a lot. However, swallowing small residues remaining in the mouth or sucking on a candy from which a small piece remains in the mouth does not invalidate the prayer. If one eats or drinks inadvertently or forgetfully, his prayer remains valid, provided that the form of the prayer is not disrupted.

Issue 342: If a person adds or subtracts intentionally or inadvertently any of the pillars of the prayer or intentionally adds or subtracts an obligatory non-pillar part, his prayer becomes invalid.

Issue 343: Saying "amīn" after reciting Sūrat al-Fātiḥah is not permissible and invalidates the prayer. However, there is no problem in doing so in a state of taqiyyah. Likewise, crossing one hand over the other in front of the body while standing in prayer invalidates it is intended as part of the prayer. It is an obligatory precaution to avoid it even without the mentioned intention.

Issue 344: Cut off an obligatory prayer without excuse is not permissible.

Issue 345: If the preservation of lives or wealth that must be preserved is jeopardized, then cutting off the prayer becomes obligatory. Generally, cutting off the prayer to ward off danger to lives and wealth recognized by the praying person is permissible.

Doubts that Arise in Prayer

Issue 346: Doubts in prayer[22] are divided into three categories:

a. Doubts regarding the essence of prayer.

b. Doubts regarding the components of prayer.

c. Doubts regarding the units [rakʿats] of prayer.

Doubts regarding the essence of prayer

Issue 347: If someone doubts after the passing of the prayer time whether he has prayed or not, or if he thinks he has prayed, then he does not need to perform the prayer. However, if such doubt occurs before the end of the prayer time, then he must perform the prayer. Moreover, even if

---

[22] Doubt (shakk) is hesitation between two or more possibilities in an equally probable way, without one being favored over the other. However, one of the possibilities has an advantage or is more likely than the others. In that case, the stronger possibility is called certainty (ẓann), while the weaker possibility is called illusion (wahm).

there is a suspicion that he has prayed, it is also obligatory for him to perform the prayer.

Doubts regarding the components of prayer:

Issue 348: If he doubts about [performing] one of the obligatory actions in prayer, and this doubt arises before entering the part immediately following it, he must perform it. However, if the doubt arises after entering the subsequent part, even if it is recommended, he should not pay attention to his doubt.

Issue 349: If he doubts whether or not he uttered Takbīrat al-Iḥrām (opening takbīr) before commencing recitation—even before seeking refuge [isti'ādhah]—he should utter it.

Issue 350: If he doubts whether he recited Sūrat al-Fātiḥah or not, and this doubt arises before entering the subsequent part, including the recommended part like saying "alḥamdulillāh Rabb al-'ālamīn," he must recite it.

Issue 351: If he doubts whether he recited the other Sūrah and has not yet entered the subsequent part, he should recite it. However, if the doubt arises after beginning with bowing, Qunūt, or the recommended remembrances after them, he should not pay attention to his doubt.

Issue 352: If he doubts whether he performed the bowing before going into prostration, he should perform it.

Issue 353: If he doubts before standing for the second or fourth unit of prayer or beginning with tashahhud, whether he performed one prostration or two, he should perform another. Similarly, he must perform a prostration if he doubts upon rising (before reaching complete standing).

Issue 354: If he doubts before raising whether he recited tashahhud or not, he should do it. However, he should not pay attention if the doubt occurs when rising. The same applies if the doubt arises after starting the subsequent part, even if it is recommended.

Issue 355: If he doubts whether he performed the salutation [taslīm] or not, and he engaged in the supplications after prayer [taʿqībāt], began with another prayer, or left the state of prayer and engaged in actions that break up its form, such as turning away from the Qiblah direction, he should not pay attention to his doubt. However, he must recite the salutation if the doubt arises before engaging in any of the mentioned actions.

Issue 356: If he is engaged in reciting a verse and doubts whether he recited the preceding verse or is occupied with reciting the last part of the verse and doubts whether he recited its beginning, he should not pay attention to his doubt.

Issue 357: If he doubts the correctness of one of the acts of prayer after completing it, he should not pay attention to his doubt, even if he has not yet entered the subsequent part.

Issue 358: If he doubts about one of the parts of prayer before entering the subsequent part, and he performs it, and afterward it becomes clear that he performed it twice, then if it was not a pillar of prayer, his prayer remains valid.

Issue 359: If he doubts about performing the preceding part after entering the subsequent part of prayer, and he does not pay attention to his doubt, then realizes that he did not perform it if he has not begun with the following pillar, he should perform it and repeat the parts he performed afterward by way of error. But if he has begun with the subsequent pillar, and the missed part was a pillar, his prayer is invalid, and if it was not [a pillar], it is valid. If the missed part was a single prostration or the tashahhud, it is obligatory to make up for the missed prostration after completing the prayer. Based on obligatory precaution, he should make up for the tashahhud and perform the two prostrations of forgetfulness.

Doubts regarding the units [rakʿats] of prayer

Issue 360: If one has doubts about the number of units in the prayer, such as not knowing whether he prayed three units or four, first, he must reflect for a moment. If he becomes certain or is strongly inclined towards one of the possibilities, he should act upon it, and his prayer remains valid. Otherwise, he should proceed according to the following rulings.

Issue 361: Doubt regarding the number of units in the prayer is divided into two categories:

1. Doubts that invalidate the prayer (invalidating doubts).
2. Doubts that do not invalidate the prayer (valid doubts).

Doubts that invalidate the prayer:

Issue 362: Doubt regarding the number of units [rakʿats] of prayer necessitates its invalidation in the following instances:

1. Doubt about the obligatory bi-unit prayers, such as the Fajr prayer and the traveler's prayer. However, doubt about the number of units in precautionary bi-unit prayers does not invalidate them.
2. Doubt about the number of units in the Maghrib prayer.
3. Doubt between the first and another unit in four-unit prayers, such as doubting between the first and second or between the first and third units.
4. Doubt between the second and another unit in four-unit prayers before completing the second

prostration, such as doubting between the second and third or between the second and fourth units.

5. Doubt about the number of units to the extent that one cannot determine how many units he prayed.

Issue 363: If the praying person experiences any of the doubts that invalidate the prayer, it is an obligatory precaution not to interrupt the prayer immediately. Rather, he must reflect until his doubt settles (meaning that he does not become certain or lean towards one possibility), and then he may interrupt the prayer.

Valid Doubts

Issue 364: If one doubts the number of units in a four-unit prayer and then his doubt changes to certainty or leaning towards one possibility, he should act upon it, complete his prayer accordingly, and his prayer is considered valid. However, if certainty or leaning towards one possibility does not occur, he should act according to the following rulings:

1. If one doubts between the second and third units after raising his head from the second prostration, he should base his action on the third unit, complete his prayer, then, after finishing, perform one precautionary unit in a standing position or

two units while sitting (the details of which will be explained later).

2. If one doubts between the second and fourth units after raising his head from the second prostration, he should base his action on the fourth unit, complete his prayer, and then, after finishing, perform two precautionary units in a standing position.

3. If one doubts between the second, third, and fourth units after raising his head from the second prostration, he should base his action on the fourth unit, complete his prayer, then, after finishing, perform two precautionary units from a standing position and two units while sitting.[23]

4. If one doubts between the third and fourth units at any point, he should base his action on the fourth unit, complete his prayer, and then, after finishing, perform one precautionary unit from a standing position or two units while sitting.

5. If one doubts between the fourth and fifth units after raising his head from the second prostration, he should base his action on the fourth unit, complete his prayer, and then, after finishing,

---

[23] Previously, it was mentioned that if any of these three doubts occur before raising the head from the second prostration, the prayer becomes invalid.

perform the two prostrations of forgetfulness (in the manner that will be explained later).

6. If one doubts between the fourth and fifth units while standing, he should base his action on the fourth unit, break his standing, sit down (without bowing), recite tashahhud, and conclude the prayer with the salutation [taslīm]. Then, after finishing, he should perform one precautionary unit from a standing position or two units while sitting.[24]

Issue 365: If one encounters one of the legitimate doubts during prayer, he must exercise caution for a while. Once his doubt settles, he should act accordingly, as previously mentioned.

Issue 366: If one encounters one of the valid doubts, it is not permissible for him to terminate the prayer. If he does so, he has sinned. If he resumes the prayer anew before committing anything that invalidates the prayer, such as turning away from the Qiblah direction, the second prayer is also invalidated. However, if he resumes the prayer anew after committing any invalidator of prayer, the second prayer is valid.

Issue 367: If one encounters doubts that necessitate performing a precautionary prayer but fails to perform it after completing the prayer and instead resumes the prayer

[24] Other instances of doubt are mentioned in detailed jurisprudential books, but encountering them is rare.

anew, he has sinned. If he resumes the prayer before committing any invalidator of prayer, the second is also invalid. However, the second is valid if he resumes the prayer after committing an invalidator of prayer.

Issue 368: Doubt regarding the number of units in prayer is considered equivalent to certainty. This means that if one is unsure whether he performed three units or four and leans towards one side, he should act based on his inclination, and his prayer remains valid.

Issue 369: If one initially leans towards one side of doubt but later becomes equally unsure (meaning both sides seem equally likely), he should act based on the doubt. If one initially doubts and before acting based on the doubt, his uncertainty shifts towards one side; he should act according to his new inclination and complete his prayer.

Precautionary Prayer [Ṣalāt al-Iḥtiyāṭ]

Issue 370: If one is obligated to perform the precautionary prayer, he must immediately proceed with the intention for the precautionary prayer and the takbīr after completing the salutation [taslīm] (without reciting the supplications after taslīm). Then, he recites Sūrat al-Fātiḥah (without the other Sūrah), bows, and then prostrates twice. If his duty is to perform one additional unit, he recites tashahhud and taslīm after the two prostrations. However, if the duty is to perform two precautionary units, he rises after the prostrations and performs another unit similar to the first, then recites the tashahhud and taslīm.

Issue 371: In the precautionary prayer, there is no recitation of another Sūrah or Qunūt, and it is not permissible to utter the intention for this prayer. Based on obligatory precaution, one must recite Sūrat al-Fātiḥah and even its bismillāh in a whisper.

Issue 372: If it becomes clear before starting the precautionary prayer that his previous prayer was valid, it is not obligatory to perform the precautionary prayer. Similarly, if it becomes clear during the precautionary prayer that it is not obligatory, it is not obligatory to complete it.

Doubts That Must Be Dismissed

Issue 373: Doubts that one must not concern himself with and must be dismissed are as follows:

1. Doubt about something after passing it.

2. Doubt after the salutation [taslīm].

3. Doubt after the passing of the prayer time.

4. Doubt of the imām (prayer leader) and the follower.

5. Doubt of the one who doubts excessively.

6. Doubt in recommended prayers.

Doubt about something after passing it:

Issue 374: If he doubts during prayer whether he has fulfilled one of the obligatory components and has already started with the subsequent part, he should not pay attention to his doubt. An example of this is if he doubts while bowing whether he recited Sūrat al-Fātiḥah or not.[25]

Doubt after the salutation [taslīm]:

Issue 375: If one doubts after the salutation whether his prayer was valid or not, such as doubting if he bowed or not, or doubting after the salutation in a four-unit prayer whether he prayed four units or five, he should not pay attention to his doubt, and he should act based on the validity of his prayer. This means that in the first scenario, he acts on the assumption that he bowed, and in the second scenario, on the assumption that he prayed four units.

Issue 376: If one doubts about the units of prayer after the salutation, and each doubt on either side is sufficient to invalidate the prayer, such as doubting after the salutation in a four-unit prayer whether he prayed three units or five, then his prayer becomes invalid.

---

[25] The rulings of this section have been covered in the topic of doubt concerning the components of prayer.

Doubt after the passing of the prayer time:

Issue 377: If one doubts whether or not he prayed after the time of prayer has passed by, then he should not concern himself with his doubt.

Doubt of the imām (prayer leader) and the follower:

Issue 378: If an imām of a congregational prayer doubts the number of rakʿahs [units of prayer]—for example, he doubts whether he has performed three rakʿahs or four rakʿahs—then, if a follower is certain or supposes that he has performed four rakʿahs and makes it known to the imām that he has performed four rakʿahs, the imām must complete the prayer, and it is not necessary for him to perform the precautionary prayer [ṣalāt al-iḥtiyāṭ]. Similarly, if the imām is certain or supposes that he has performed a certain number of rakʿahs and a follower doubts the number of rakʿahs, the follower must dismiss his doubt.

Doubt of the one who doubts excessively:

Issue 379: One who habitually has doubts three times in one single prayer, or if three consecutive prayers are not free from his doubt at least once, and if the frequency of his doubt is not due to some extraneous cause necessitating fear, anger, or a disturbance of the senses, then he is characterized as having excessive doubt, and he must thus dismiss his doubts.

Issue 380: If one frequently doubts about performing a certain act, and if performing that act does not invalidate the prayer, he should assume that he performed it. For example, if he doubts whether he prostrated or not, he should assume that he did. However, if performing that act invalidates the prayer, he should assume that he did not perform it. For example, if he doubts whether he performed one or more bowings, he must assume that he performed only one, as adding bowings in prayer invalidates it.

Issue 381: If one's frequent doubt is specific to a particular part of the prayer, the ruling of excessive doubt applies only to that part. If doubt arises about other parts of the prayer, he should act according to his doubt. For instance, if someone frequently doubts during prostration and then doubts about performing the bowing, he should act according to his doubt. So, if he is standing, he should perform the bowing, but if he is in prostration, he should dismiss his doubt.

Issue 382: If one frequently has doubts about a particular prayer, such as prayers offered aloud, for example, then if he has doubts about other prayers, such as prayers offered in a whisper, he must act according to his doubt.

Issue 383: If someone frequently has doubts during prayer in a specific place and then prays in a different place where he has doubts, he should act according to his doubts.

Issue 384: If a person doubts whether he is experiencing a state of excessive doubt, he should assume that he is not experiencing it. If the one prone to excessive doubt is not certain that he has returned to the state of ordinary individuals, he must not pay attention to his doubts.

Doubt in recommended prayers:

Issue 385: If a person doubts the number of rakʿahs [units of prayer] he has performed in a recommended prayer if the greater of the two numbers he is doubtful about would invalidate the prayer, he must assume the lesser number is correct. For example, in the Fajr recommended prayer [the ṣubḥ nafl], if one doubts whether he has performed two rakʿahs or three rakʿahs, he must assume he has performed two rakʿahs. However, if the greater of the two numbers would not invalidate the prayer—for example, he doubts whether he has performed two rakʿahs or one rakʿah—then his prayer is valid whichever side of the doubt he acts upon.

Issue 386: If one doubts one of the components of a recommended prayer, whether it is a pillar part [rukn] or not, and he has not moved past the point of that component, he must perform it. But if he has moved past that point, he should not pay attention to his doubt.

Issue 387: Adding a pillar of prayer in a recommended prayer does not invalidate it, but omitting a pillar component invalidates the prayer based on obligatory precaution. If one forgets a part of the recommended prayer and remembers that after starting with the next pillar of prayer, he must perform the missed part and repeat the subsequent part. For example, if he remembers during bowing that he did not recite the other Sūrah, he should return to recite the Sūrah and then repeat the bowing.

Prostration of Forgetfulness

Issue 388: After the salutation [taslīm], it is obligatory for the worshiper to perform the two prostrations of forgetfulness (in the manner to be explained later) in three cases:

1. Speaking inadvertently during the prayer.

2. Doubting whether one performed four or five units in a four-unit prayer after completing the second prostration.

3. Forgetting to recite tashahhud.

And it is obligatory, based on precaution, to perform the two prostrations of forgetfulness in two cases:

4. Forgetting one prostration.

5. Reciting taslīm inadvertently outside its designated place (at the end).

Issue 389: Based on recommended precaution, the worshiper should perform the two prostrations of forgetfulness for every addition or deficiency (except for the mentioned cases) due to forgetfulness in the prayer, which he realizes after moving past it, such as if he inadvertently forgets the four tasbīhs and remembers during the bowing or after it.

Speaking inadvertently during the prayer:

Issue 390: It is obligatory to perform the two prostrations of forgetfulness if one speaks inadvertently or because he thought his prayer has finished.

Issue 391: Involuntary utterances or sounds due to sighing or coughing do not necessitate prostration of forgetfulness. However, if one groans or says "oh" inadvertently, then performing the two prostrations of forgetfulness is obligatory.

Issue 392: If one makes a mistake in reciting a word and corrects it properly, there is no obligation for him to perform the prostration of forgetfulness for the correction.

Issue 393: If one speaks several words inadvertently during the prayer, then if it counts as one occurrence, performing the prostration of forgetfulness once is sufficient.

Reciting taslīm inadvertently outside its designated place (at the end):

Issue 394: If one inadvertently recites either of the two forms of the salutation—"assalāmu ʿalaynā wa ʿalā ʿibādil lāhiṣ ṣāliḥīn" or "assalāmu ʿalaykum wa raḥmatul lāhi wa barakātuh"—outside of its designated place (which is at the end of the prayer), it is obligatory precaution to perform the two prostrations of forgetfulness. However, if one inadvertently recites only a portion of the salutation, then it is recommended precaution to perform the two prostrations of forgetfulness.

Issue 395: If one inadvertently recites the three expressions of salutation outside its designated place, it suffices to perform the two prostrations of forgetfulness once.

Forgetting a prostration or tashahhud:

Issue 396: If one forgets tashahhud or one prostration and remembers before bowing for the next unit of prayer, he must promptly proceed to sit and perform the missed prostration or tashahhud.

Issue 397: If one forgets one prostration or tashahhud and remembers during the bowing of the following unit of prayer or afterward, it is obligatory, after the salutation, to make up for the missed prostration and after that, based on obligatory precaution, he should perform the two prostrations of forgetfulness. Based on obligatory precaution, in the event of forgetfulness, one must also make up for the tashahhud and then perform the two prostrations of forgetfulness.

Method of Performing the Prostration of Forgetfulness

Issue 398: To perform the prostration of forgetfulness, it is necessary—after the reciting the salutation [taslīm]—to promptly place the forehead on what is permissible to prostrate on with the intention of performing the prostration of forgetfulness, and it is an obligatory precaution for one to say: "Bismil lāhi wa billāhi, assalāmu ʿalayka ayyuhan nabiyyu wa raḥmatul lāhi wa barakātuh" [In the name of God, and by God. Peace be upon you, O Prophet, and the mercy of God and His blessings (be upon you too)]. Then, he should raise his head from prostration, prostrate again, repeat the remembrance, and then recite tashahhud and taslīm.

Rulings of the Prostration of Forgetfulness

Issue 399: If one deliberately neglects to perform the prostration of forgetfulness after the salutation, he must promptly commence with it as soon as possible. However, if he forgets, he must perform it immediately upon recollection. In any case, there is no obligation to repeat the prayer.

Making Up For a Missed Prostration and Tashahhud

Issue 400: If one inadvertently omits any non-pillar (non-rukn) part of the prayer, his prayer does not become invalid, and it is only obligatory to make up for it in the case of a missed prostration and, based on obligatory precaution, a missed tashahhud. Both should be made up for after completing the prayer.

Issue 401: If one advertently skips a prostration and remembers it during the bowing of the subsequent unit of prayer or thereafter, it is obligatory to make up for it after completing the prayer.

Issue 402: If one forgets to recite tashahhud and remembers it during the bowing of the subsequent unit of prayer or thereafter, his prayer does not become invalid. Based on obligatory precaution, he must make up for the missed tashahhud after completing the prayer.

Issue 403: It is necessary, in making up for the prostration and tashahhud that were missed, to observe all the conditions of the prayer, such as bodily and clothing purity, facing the Qiblah, and other conditions.

Issue 404: There is no obligation to recite taslīm after making up for the missed tashahhud, and likewise, there is no obligation to recite tashahhud and taslīm after making up for the missed prostration.

Issue 405: If one commits an act that invalidates the prayer between the taslīm of the prayer and the making up of the prostration or tashahhud, such as deviating from the Qiblah, he must make up for the prostration and tashahhud, and his prayer remains valid.

Issue 406: If one is obligated to make up for prostration or tashahhud, and he is also obligated to perform the prostration of forgetfulness for another matter, he must first make up for the prostration or tashahhud after completing the prayer and then perform the prostrations of forgetfulness for the other matter.

Prayers of a Traveler

Issue 407: It is obligatory for the traveler to offer the obligatory four-unit daily prayers (i.e., Ẓuhr, 'Aṣr, and 'Ishā') in their shortened form ["qaṣr" prayers] by omitting the last two units of each prayer if the conditions for shortening are met. [From this point henceforth, we will use the term "perform qaṣr prayers" to refer to the shortening of prayers, and "perform tamām [full, complete] prayers" to refer to the normal performing of prayers, i.e., all four units.]

Issue 408: The conditions for shortening prayers during travel are eight:

1. The distance prescribed by Islāmic law.

2. The intention is to cover the distance prescribed by Islāmic law.

3. Continuity of intention (not changing the intention to cover the distance and not wavering in it).

4. Not passing by one's hometown and not intending to stay [in a place] for more than ten days during the journey.

5. Travel should not be undertaken for unlawful purposes.

6. The traveler should not be one of those whose homes are with them (will be explained later).

7. Travel should not be a [regular] part of work.

8. Reaching the outer limit (ḥadd al-tarakhkhuṣ) for allowing shortening the prayers.

First Condition: The Distance Prescribed by Islāmic Law

Issue 409: The condition for shortening prayers is that the distance traveled must not be less than 8 Farasikh. Prayers should not be shortened if the journey is less than this distance.

Issue 410: The distance prescribed by Islāmic law (8 Farasikh) that requires shortening prayers (according to the study conducted, which provides reassurance and certainty on the matter) is equivalent to 41 kilometers.

Issue 411: The measurement of the prescribed distance includes the distance between the end boundary of the land of departure and the beginning boundary of the land of arrival, whether the land is a major land or not.

Issue 412: If the traveler's destination is not the city itself but a specific and independent location on the outskirts of the city, where entering the city and passing through it is not considered by custom ['urf] as arrival to the destination, but rather entering the city and passing through it is considered a means to reach the destination, such as some universities, military camps, or hospitals located on the outskirts of cities, then the distance is calculated to the specific intended location, not to the beginning boundary of the city.

Issue 413: Traveling the prescribed distance required to shorten the prayer consecutively is unnecessary. Rather, traveling this distance in a non-consecutive manner also necessitates shortening it.

Issue 414: The distance is considered consecutive if the distance from the origin to the destination or from the destination to the origin is at least eight Farasikh (41 kilometers). The distance is considered non-consecutive if each of the distances from the origin to the destination and from the destination to the origin is less than eight Farasikh and the total of the round trip is at least eight Farasikh.

Issue 415: In the non-consecutive distance, the distance of the outward journey must not be less than twenty-five and a half kilometers. Therefore, if his outward journey is five Farasikh and his return journey is three Farasikh, the traveler should perform qaṣr prayers. However, suppose his outward journey is three Farasikh, and his return journey is five Farasikh. In that case, he should perform tamām prayers unless the return journey alone is eight Farasikh or more, in which case he should perform qaṣr prayers from the beginning of the journey.

Issue 416: In the non-consecutive journey, it is not a condition that he return on the same day or night. Even if he stays for several days and then returns, he remains in the state of shortening prayer unless he encounters what breaks his travel conditions, such as intending to stay for ten days in one place. Similarly, the traveler should perform qaṣr prayers in the case of consecutive distance if he intends to stay for several days in a place before reaching the eight Farasikh without any of the disrupters of travel occurring.

Issue 417: If he travels a distance of less than four Farasikh, such as one and a half Farasikh, several times back and forth, so that the total distance is eight Farasikh or more, he should not perform qaṣr prayers.

Issue 418: If the traveler has multiple destinations, and going to the next destination requires going back part of the distance he has traveled, then if the distance from the origin to the final destination (considering the amount of distance he has returned to go to the next destination) is not less than eight Farasikh in the consecutive journey, and four Farasikh in the non-consecutive journey, so that the total is not less than eight Farasikh, he should perform qaṣr prayers even if the total distance without considering the amount he returned is less than eight Farasikh.

Issue 419: If there are two ways to reach the destination, one long and not less than eight Farasikh, and the other short and less than eight Farasikh, several scenarios can be imagined:

1. If he goes by the long way, he should perform qaṣr prayers, whether he intends to return in the same way or not.

2. If he goes by the short way and it is not less than four Farasikh, he should perform qaṣr prayers, whether he intends to return in the same way.

3. If the short way is less than four Farasikh and he wants to go by it and return by the long way, he should perform qaṣr prayers.

4. If the short way is less than four Farasikh and he wants to go and return by it, he should perform tamām prayers.

Issue 420: In the case of the previous issue, if each of the two ways is less than eight Farasikh, then if one of them is at least four Farasikh, and the traveler goes by it, and the total of the outward and return journey is at least eight Farasikh, he should perform qaṣr prayers. Otherwise, he should perform tamām prayer.

Issue 421: If the distance of eight Farasikh is circular outside the city and after passing the outer limit (ḥadd al-tarakhkhuṣ) for allowing shortening the prayers, and he does not have a specific destination on this road, but the purpose is to walk on it, such as if he takes it to inspect the condition of the road or to train his car, then in this case, the distance is considered consecutive, and he should perform qaṣr prayers.

Ways to Establish the Legal Distance

Issue 422: If he knows or is certain that the distance of his journey is at least eight Farasikh, or two just witnesses testify to that, then he should perform qaṣr prayers.

Issue 423: If the common and widespread opinion among people leads to knowledge or certainty of the realization of the prescribed distance, it can be relied upon, and the prayers should thus be shortened. However, in other cases, it is not considered even if it leads to suspicion.

Issue 424: If the traveler is doubtful about reaching the distance, and if the investigation into this does not entail hardship, such as checking the car's kilometer counter or asking several people, for example, then it is an obligatory precaution to investigate. If he does not reach a result, he should perform tamām prayers.

Issue 425: If the follower does not know the verdict of his marjaʿ [the Āyatullāh he emulates], such as if he is ignorant of his verdict regarding the non-consecutive distance, whether it is the same as the consecutive distance or not, then he must investigate the verdict of his marjaʿ. If he cannot investigate or does not want to do so, he must practice caution by performing both qaṣr and tamām prayers.

Issue 426: If someone must perform tamām prayers due to doubt about the distance if he performs qaṣr prayers contrary to his duty, then his prayer is insufficient and must be repeated in full. Yes, if it becomes clear after the prayer that his duty is shortening it, then if he has performed it with the intention of closeness, it is sufficient, and he does not have to repeat it.

Issue 427: If he believes that the distance between the origin and the destination is in line with the prescribed distance and prays shortened, then it becomes clear that it is less than the prescribed distance, then he must repeat the prayer completely in time and make it up outside of it.

Issue 428: If he believes that the distance he traveled is less than eight Farasikh, so he offers prayer in full (complete), then it becomes clear that it is equivalent to the prescribed distance, then he must repeat the prayer shortened [qaṣr] if the time of prayer has still not passed and make up for it if the time of prayer has passed.

Issue 429: If someone intends to go to a specific place and doubts whether the way to it covers the prescribed distance or believes that it is less than the prescribed distance, his duty in both cases is to perform tamām prayers. Then, if it is proven to him during the journey that it covers the prescribed distance, he should perform qaṣr prayers from that place, and the distance from the point where he gained knowledge to the destination does not have to be a prescribed distance.

Second Condition: Intention to Cover the Distance Prescribed by Islāmic law:

Issue 430: When leaving the city, the accountable person [mukallaf] must intend to travel eight Farasikh (consecutive or non-consecutive). Therefore, if he initially intends to go less than the prescribed distance, such as if he intends to travel three Farasikh, for example, and after reaching the destination (three Farasikh), he intends to travel another five Farasikh to stay there for ten days, then such a journey does not necessitate shortening the prayer even though he traveled eight Farasikh.

Issue 431: If someone does not know how far he wants to travel when he starts the journey, such as a policeman tasked with arresting a criminal, and he does not know whether he will travel eight Farasikh (consecutive or non-consecutive) or not, then he should not shorten his prayer even if he travels eight Farasikh. Yes, if the return distance is eight Farasikh, he should shorten the prayer on the return journey. Similarly, if he learns during the journey that he must travel another four Farasikh so that it becomes eight Farasikh with the return journey, he should perform qaṣr prayers from that place.

Issue 432: Knowing that one has traveled the prescribed distance is like intending to cover the distance. Therefore, if he knows that he will cover the prescribed distance in his travel, it serves the role of intention, and he should thus perform qaṣr prayers.

Issue 433: If he intends to travel the prescribed distance, he should perform qaṣr prayers even if he does not specify a specific place.

Issue 434: The intention to cover the prescribed distance must be definite. Therefore, if the journey is conditional on the occurrence of an event, the prayer is not shortened. An example is if a person intends to go to a place less than four Farasikh away so that if he finds someone there to accompany him, he will complete his journey; otherwise, he will return. His intention is not definite in this case, and he should perform tamām prayers.

Issue 435: In the previous case, if he knows that he will find someone to accompany him, then in reality, he has intended eight Farasikh, and he should perform qaṣr prayers after passing the outer limit (ḥadd al-tarakhkhuṣ).

Issue 436: If someone wants to travel eight Farasikh, but he will stay for ten days in one place during the journey (before reaching eight Farasikh), he should perform tamām prayers. Yes, suppose he changes his mind about staying for ten days after traveling part of the distance. In that case, if the remaining amount covers a prescribed distance, even if it is non-consecutive, and the remaining amount of the outward journey is at least four Farasikh, or the return journey alone is eight Farasikh, he should perform qaṣr prayers. Otherwise, he offers his prayers in full (complete).

Issue 437: In the consecutive distance, if he is hesitant whether to intend to stay for ten days in a place on the way before reaching eight Farasikh or not, then he does not intend to travel the prescribed distance, so he should perform tamām prayers.

Issue 438: In the non-consecutive distance, if he is hesitant whether to intend to stay for ten days at the destination or before it, or after it on the return journey before traveling eight Farasikh or not, then the intention of covering eight Farasikh is not realized, so he should perform tamām prayers.

Issue 439: Traveling the distance continuously without stopping is not obligatory. If someone intends to travel the prescribed distance, if he stays for a night or two in a place after traveling two or three Farasikh, then travels another part of the distance, then stays for several nights, then as long as he does not intend to stay for ten days in one place, he should perform qaṣr prayers.

Rulings of following in travel

Issue 440: A follower in travel, whether the following is voluntary or obligatory, should perform qaṣr prayers if he knows that the one he is following in travel [the followed] intends to travel a prescribed distance.

Issue 441: If the follower does not know whether the followed intends to travel a prescribed distance, he is not obligated to ask him, and he followed is not obligated to inform the follower. If the follower does not know the intention of the followed for the prescribed distance, he should perform tamām prayers.

Issue 442: If the follower believes that the followed does not intend to cover the prescribed distance, then learns during the journey that he does intend it, then if the remaining part of the journey is less than the prescribed distance (consecutive or non-consecutive), he should perform tamām prayers.

Issue 443: If a person is taken to a place without his choice and knows they will travel eight Farasikh with him, he should perform qaṣr prayers.

Third Condition: Continuity of Intention to Cover the Prescribed Distance:

Issue 444: The third condition of shortening the prayer is continuing the intention to cover the prescribed distance. Suppose the aforementioned condition is not met during the journey. In that case, he should perform tamām prayers even if all the other conditions are met, such as if he intends to travel eight Farasikh, and after traveling two or three Farasikh, he changes his mind about continuing the journey or hesitates about it, but he loses his way and continues his journey to the same place of eight Farasikh. He offers his prayer in full (complete) in this case.

Issue 445: If he intends at the beginning of the journey to go to a specific place that is eight Farasikh away, but before reaching four Farasikh, he decides to go to another place that is also eight Farasikh away from the beginning of his journey, then he should perform qaṣr prayers.

Issue 446: If someone intends to travel eight Farasikh consecutively, and after reaching four Farasikh, he changes his mind and decides to return the same way (meaning that he converts the consecutive distance to a non-consecutive one), he should perform qaṣr prayers.

Issue 447: If someone intends to travel eight Farasikh or more, changes his mind, or hesitates before reaching four Farasikh, he should perform tamām prayers. However, if he returns to the previous intention and intends to continue the journey, there are several cases:

1. Suppose he stops at a specific place while he is in a state of hesitation or change of mind about continuing the journey. In that case, he should perform qaṣr prayers, whether the remaining part of the journey covers a prescribed distance alone or less. Even if he wants to pray in that place after

making the intention again and before traveling, he should perform qaṣr prayers.

2. If he travels a distance after hesitation or a change of mind about continuing the journey, and the remaining part of the journey covers a prescribed distance (consecutive or non-consecutive), then in this case, he should perform tamām prayers during the distance he traveled while hesitating. However, after making the intention, he should perform qaṣr prayers again.

3. If he travels a distance after hesitation or a change of mind about continuing the journey, and the remaining part is less than the prescribed distance, he should perform tamām prayers. Yes, if the total distance before the change of mind or hesitation and after making the intention to continue the journey again is a prescribed distance, then the obligatory precaution, in this case, is to combine the shortening and completion of prayers.

Issue 448: If someone travels intending to cover the prescribed distance and shortens his prayers after passing the outer limit (ḥadd al-tarakhkhuṣ) for allowing shortening the prayers if he changes his mind before reaching four Farasikh or makes the intention to stay for ten days, then the obligatory precaution is for him to repeat the prayers he performed shortened if the time of prayer has not yet passed and make them up if the time of prayer has passed.

Fourth Condition: Not Passing Through One's Hometown [waṭan] or a Place of Residence [of ten days]:

Issue 449: One of the conditions of shortening the prayer is that one does not intend, from the beginning of the journey or during it, to stay in a place for ten days during the journey and before reaching eight Farasikh or to pass by one's hometown as well.

Issue 450: If he intends at the beginning of the journey or during it to stay in a place for ten days or to pass by his hometown before reaching eight Farasikh, he should perform tamām prayers from the beginning. Similarly, he should perform tamām prayers if the remaining distance after leaving the hometown or place of residence [of ten days] is less than eight Farasikh, even if it is non-consecutive.

Issue 451: In the case of the previous issue, if he is hesitant about staying for ten days in a place or passing by his hometown during the journey, then the intention of covering the prescribed distance is not realized, so he should perform tamām prayers.

Fifth Condition: The Travel Should Not Be for an Unlawful Purpose:

Issue 452: Another condition of shortening the prayer in travel is that the journey must be for a permissible purpose (not unlawful). Therefore, if his journey is for a sinful purpose, whether the journey itself is forbidden, such as fleeing from jihad, or to do something forbidden, such as theft, then he should perform tamām prayers.

Issue 453: If the journey necessitates abandoning an obligatory act, then if his intention from the journey is to abandon the obligatory act, such as avoiding the payment of a debt, he should perform tamām prayers. However, if his intention was not to abandon the obligatory act—and if the leaving happens involuntarily—then the journey is not a sin, and he should perform qaṣr prayers.

Issue 454: If he travels using a usurped vehicle or crosses over a usurped land, it is not considered a journey of sin, and he should perform qaṣr prayers, although the obligatory precaution is to combine [both shortening and completion].

Issue 455: If he follows a tyrant in his journey, is forced and compelled to follow him, or if his goal is permissible and outweighs the sin, such as preventing the tyrant's injustice, he should perform qaṣr prayers. However, if he follows him of his own free will and for an unlawful purpose, or not for an unlawful purpose, it necessitates strengthening the tyrant's power or helping him in his injustice. The journey is a sin, and he must fully offer his prayers (complete).

Issue 456: If he doubts whether his journey is unlawful or not, he should assume the absence of prohibition and thus shorten his prayers, unless this journey was previously a sin, and he now doubts whether it is still unlawful or not, in which case he assumes the prohibition of the journey and offers his prayers in full (complete).

Continued Permissibility of the Travel

Issue 457: The condition of the permissibility of travel for shortening the prayer is not limited to the beginning of the journey only, but it must be met throughout the journey. Therefore, if the traveler changes his mind to sin during the journey, the journey becomes a sin, and he must offer his prayers in full (complete), even if he has traveled a prescribed distance.

Issue 458: If he began a permissible journey and shortened his prayers on the way (before reaching eight Farasikh) according to his duty, then changed his mind to an unlawful purpose for the journey, he must repeat the prayers he shortened, offering them in full (complete) if the time for the prayer has not yet passed, or make them up if the time for the prayer has passed.[26]

---

[26] As for whether he changed his intention after reaching eight Farasikh, the prayers he performed shortened remain valid.

Issue 459: If he traveled a permissible journey, and after reaching the destination, he intended a new unlawful journey (such as if he returned home to flee from war). In this case, he should perform tamām prayers from when he intended the sin (to flee from the front). However, the obligatory precaution is to combine the shortening and completion of prayers from when he intended the sin until he starts the journey.

Issue 460: If he started the journey with the intention of the permissible, then changed his mind to a sinful intention in the place where he stopped after traveling the prescribed distance, then if he wants to pray before starting the journey, he offers his prayers in full (complete), although the obligatory precaution is also to combine complete and shortened.

Issue 461: If he started the journey with the intention of the permissible, then changed to a sinful intention after traveling part of the distance, and covered part of the way with this intention, then changed again to a permissible intention, then if the total distance he traveled—without the distance he traveled with the intention of the sin—is eight Farasikh, he should perform qaṣr prayers at most.

Issue 462: If he traveled for a permissible purpose, such as trade or tourism, but traveled part of the way with the intention of sin along with the intention of the permissible, then he must offer his prayers in full (complete) in the part that he travels with the intention of both the unlawful and the permissible, although the recommended precaution is also to shorten his prayers. However, in the remaining part of the journey, in which he intends only the permissible if it covers a prescribed distance (even with the addition of the first part that he traveled with the intention of the permissible), he should perform qaṣr prayers.

Issue 463: If he intended the sin at the beginning of the journey, if he changed his mind during the journey and decided to continue his journey for a permissible purpose, then if the remaining part of the journey is eight Farasikh (consecutive or non-consecutive), he should perform qaṣr prayers. However, in other cases, he should perform tamām prayers. If the return alone is eight Farasikh, he should perform qaṣr prayers from when he intended the permissible again.

Issue 464: In the case of the previous issue, if he changed his mind about his sinful intention in the place where he stopped and wanted to pray there (before the journey), he should perform tamām prayers, although the recommended precaution in this case is to combine shortening and completion of prayers.

Issue 465: Traveling for recreation and tourism is permissible, and shortening prayers on such travels is obligatory.

Issue 466: In the journey for the purpose of sin, the recommended prayers [nawāfil] of Ẓuhr, ʿAṣr, and ʿIshāʾ can still be performed.

Issue 467: In the journey of sin, attendance at Friday prayer is not dropped.

Returning From a Travel of Sin

Issue 468: The one returning from a journey of sin, if his return journey covers a prescribed distance and the journey itself (not its destination) was unlawful, and the return from the journey of sin is a continuation of the same journey, then in the case of repentance, he should perform qaṣr prayers. But if he does not repent, the obligatory precaution is to combine shortening and completing prayers. However, if the purpose of his journey was unlawful, the obligatory precaution is to combine the shortening and completion of prayers whether he repents or not. However, if the return is considered a new journey (and not a continuation of the previous journey), such as if he wanted to return to his first country after a year, for example, then in any case (whether he repents or not), he must shorten his prayers and break his fast.

Traveling for Hunting

Issue 469: Traveling to hunt for food for oneself, one's family, and their other needs is permissible, and one should perform qaṣr prayers on such travels.

Issue 470: If the journey is for hunting for trade and profit, such as someone who hunts animals to sell their meat, skins, teeth, and other parts, i.e., for trade and gaining wealth and ample profit,[27] In this case, the obligatory precaution is to combine shortening and completion. However, this does not apply to fasting (he must break his fast).

Issue 471: If the hunting travel is for diversion purposes,[28] (and not to eat, secure livelihood, or trade), then one must offer his prayers in full (complete) and fast.

Issue 472: A recreational journey in which one eats the meat of what he hunts does not fall under the ruling of a journey for diversion purposes.

Sixth Condition: The Traveler Should Have a Permanent Home:

Issue 473: One of the conditions for shortening the prayer in travel is that the person has a place of stability and a fixed

---

[27] This means that if one sells the animals he hunts for livelihood, then, in this case, prayers during such hunting travels are shortened. However, if the purpose of hunting is not to meet livelihood needs but rather to acquire abundant wealth, such as hunting rare animals like the cheetah, squirrel, or elephant to sell ivory, hides, or other parts of the animal to accumulate wealth, then in this case, prayers are not shortened during the hunting trip.

[28] This means hunting animals for recreation, regardless of whether they are edible.

point of residence outside of travel. Therefore, if the traveler does not have any fixed place, place of stability, or residence (meaning that he is one of those whose homes are with them),[29] he should perform tamām prayers.

Issue 474: Badawī (Bedouin) tribes who live in one place for part of the year and travel to Badawī areas in the other part of the year and settle in mountainous or plain areas are not considered those whose homes are with them. Rather, they are those who have two homelands. Therefore, if the distance between the two places is prescribed, they shorten their prayers on the way.

Issue 475: If someone whose home is with him wants to travel another journey, such as if he wants to go on pilgrimage, or if he wants to go to another country to visit a sick person, then if in this journey also—like all his other journeys—he takes his family and everything that he usually takes with him on his journeys, so that the title "those whose homes are with them" applies to him during this period as well, then he should perform tamām prayers. However, if he leaves them in one country and travels alone so that the notion that his home is with him does not apply to him during that period, then the obligation to shorten prayers is not far-fetched.

---

[29] The expression "those whose homes are with them" refers to travelers who carry their household belongings and means of livelihood with them but do not have a fixed dwelling, home, or specific place where they settle so that when they leave, they return to it.

Issue 476: If he settles in a specific place for part of the year, but in the other part, he does not have a fixed place, but his home is with him, then he should perform tamām prayers in the place of settlement. However, when he leaves and is not settled in one place (like some tribes), the obligatory precaution is to combine the shortening and completion of prayers.

Issue 477: If a person separates from a tribe of those whose homes are with them to search for water and grass, he should perform tamām prayers even if he travels eight Farasikh or more.

Seventh Condition: The travel Should Not Be Part of His Work:

Issue 478: One of the conditions of shortening the prayer in travel is that the travel must not be for work. Therefore, if it is work, whether the traveler's job is based on travel, such as driving a car or an airplane, or whether the travel is a prelude to the job, such as a doctor or a teacher who travels for work, then he should perform tamām prayers and his fasting remains valid in that journey.

Issue 479: If his job is not travel-based, he should perform qaṣr prayers even if he travels repeatedly, whether he intends multiple journeys from the beginning, such as someone who intends to travel from Tehrān to Jamkarān Mosque forty Fridays or he travels repeatedly by chance and without intention, such as a patient who is forced to travel repeatedly to a city for treatment.

Issue 480: For travel to be considered a work trip, three conditions must be met:

1. Intention to establish a work trip.

2. Starting the work trip.

3. Intention to continue and persevere on the work trip.

Issue 481: The criterion for whether a journey is a work journey is based on custom [ʿurf]. Therefore, in case of doubt about whether the profession and work are considered by ʿurf as travel, he should perform qaṣr prayers, and his fasting is not valid.

Issue 482: It is not considered a work trip. It is for earning money and earning a living. For a teacher who travels to teach for free, this is considered a job and profession, and he must thus offer his prayers in full (complete) in his journey.

Issue 483: After fulfilling the above conditions, the ruling of travel applies from the first work trip, so he must offer his prayers in full (complete), and his fasting is valid.

Issue 484: If traveling to acquire knowledge is part of the profession and work, such as if a training course is held for an employee who travels to attend it, he should perform tamām prayers.

Issue 485: As for a university student or a student who travels to acquire knowledge in order to be able to choose a job for himself in the future, the obligatory precaution in his journey for study is to combine shortening and completion of prayers, as well fasting at the time and making up later.

Issue 486: If the acquisition of knowledge is combined with entering a group that is considered a profession, such as a student of religious sciences who is considered a "man of religion" from the beginning of his studies or students of the military college who are given a military rank after training and studying for several months in the university and are called "officers," then this type of study is considered part of the profession and work, and they must offer their prayers in full (complete) and fast in their journey to study.

Issue 487: If the accountable person wants to establish a single long work trip, such as a long sea voyage, such that it is not far-fetched to be considered a work trip by custom, then he should perform tamām prayers on such a trip, even if he did not intend to continue and persevere on it, meaning that a single long trip serves as a substitute for the intention to continue.

Issue 488: If someone wants to work on something for a single time in a year for a month, for example, such as a pilgrimage tour leader, if he wants to continue working this job every year, then he should perform tamām prayers even in the first journey. However, if he does not intend to continue, he should perform qaṣr prayers.

Issue 489: If someone travels for work in one part of the year, intending to continue and persevere in this work every year, such as a driver who works for a month or two in the summer, then his journey is considered a work journey, and he should perform tamām prayers from the first journey.

Issue 490: If someone wants to work once in a part of the year without the intention of continuing and persevering in it in the coming years, then if the duration of the work is at least three months customarily and continuously (meaning that he does not stop working except on customary holidays, such as holidays and in mourning periods), then he should perform tamām prayers even in the first journey. However, if his work period is not long, such as if he wants to work for a month, for example, and it is unclear whether it can be considered work travel by custom, then in case of doubt, he should perform qaṣr prayers.

Issue 491: If someone's job is to commute outside the city, covering a distance that is less than the prescribed distance, such as some taxi drivers, if he happens to travel for the same job for a prescribed distance, the ruling of a work trip does not apply to him, and he should perform qaṣr prayers.

Issue 492: If someone's job is to travel (whether his job is based on travel or travel is a prelude to his job), if he establishes a non-work trip, he should perform qaṣr prayers even if his journey is to his workplace.

Issue 493: In the case of the previous issue, if he establishes a non-work trip to his workplace and then intends to stay there for work, he should perform tamām prayers during his stay at work and also afterward and on the way back, although the recommended precaution is to combine shortening and completion of prayers during the stay to go to work.

Issue 494: If someone's job is travel-based if he stays in his hometown[30] or elsewhere for ten days—whether the stay is intended or not—he should not shorten his prayers in the first journey afterward.

Issue 495: If someone's job is travel-based, if he stays for ten days in his hometown or elsewhere and then establishes a non-work trip afterward, such as if he travels for Ziyārah, for example, then the obligatory precaution in the work trip that follows the Ziyārah trip is to combine shortening and completion of prayers.

---

30 To review the rulings related to the hometown, see issues 527 and 557.

Issue 496: If someone's job is travel-based, if he doubts that he stayed in a place for ten days or less, then if his doubt stems from doubt about the day of arrival at that place, he should perform tamām prayers in the first work trip. However, if his doubt stems from doubt about the day of departure, he should perform qaṣr prayers in it.

Issue 497: If someone's job is travel-based, and he has one destination in his work trip and stays for ten days in one place on the way, then the remaining part of the way to the destination, along with the way back to the hometown, is considered the first travel, and he should perform qaṣr prayers in it.

Issue 498: In the case of the previous issue, if he has multiple destinations, then the first work trip (after staying for ten days) ends upon arrival at the first destination, and from the moment of departure towards the second destination, the second journey begins, and he should perform tamām prayers.

Issue 499: On a work trip in which he should perform tamām prayers and fasting is valid; the ruling does not differ whether the previous path is the same or not, and the same about the type of work and the means of transportation.

Issue 500: If someone's job is driving, and his car breaks down after he starts driving, and he travels a prescribed distance to repair it and buy spare parts, then this journey is also considered a work journey, and one should perform tamām prayers in it.

Issue 501: In the case of the previous issue, if his car breaks down before starting work, and he travels a prescribed distance to repair it or to buy spare parts, then he should perform qaṣr prayers.

Issue 502: If someone's job is travel-based, if he establishes a non-work trip, then he must perform qaṣr prayer as someone whose job is to transport passengers from one city to another; if he travels to pilgrimage or the holy shrines, he should perform qaṣr prayer. However, if he has personal work in addition to the work trip, such as a Ziyārah, for example—whether the original purpose of the trip is personal, and transporting passengers is secondary, or vice versa, or the two purposes are equal—then he should perform tamām prayers.

Issue 503: If someone's job is travel-based, if he establishes a non-work trip, and he wants to go from there to the workplace, if he does not stay in that place for ten days (whether intended or not), he should perform tamām prayers in his journey to the workplace.

Issue 504: If someone's job is travel-based, he should perform tamām prayer on the way back from the work trip. However, if he stays there for several days (less than ten days) for non-work purposes, such as Ziyārah or sightseeing, and then returns, then the obligatory precaution is to perform both qaṣr and tamām prayers on the way back.

Issue 505: If someone's job is travel-based, if he travels the last work trip or decides to stop working permanently during the trip, then if the travel is essential for his work, such as driving a car, for example, then in this case if he does not take passengers on the way back from the last trip, his return is not considered a work trip and he should perform qaṣr prayers in it, whether he returns by his car or by another means of transportation. However, if the travel is a prelude to his work, the obligatory precaution on the way back from the last trip is to perform both qaṣr and tamām prayers.

Eighth Condition: Reaching the Outer Limit for Allowing Shortening the Prayers:

Issue 506: The traveler who leaves his hometown intending to cover the prescribed distance must perform qaṣr prayers upon reaching a specific point, and the same during the return journey; he must perform tamām prayers upon reaching that point on the way back. This point is termed "the outer limit" (ḥadd al-tarakhkhuṣ)[31] for allowing the shortening of the prayers. It is recommended to perform both qaṣr and tamām prayers within the distance between the outer limit and the hometown.

---

[31] Based on conducted research, the limit of tarkhuṣ is approximately 1,350 meters from the last point of the city.

Issue 507: The criterion for determining ḥadd al-tarakhkhuṣ is for the traveler to move away from the last houses of the city until he reaches a point where he can no longer hear the known call to prayer [ādhān] of the city without a loudspeaker, whether the walls of the city are visible or not.

Issue 508: If the traveler hears the call to prayer outside the city but is unable to distinguish between its different parts, it is an obligatory precaution to perform both qaṣr and tamām prayers unless he continues his journey until he can no longer hear the call to prayer at all.

Issue 509: The criterion for the outer limit (ḥadd al-tarakhkhuṣ) is to hear the call to prayer raised from a recognizable elevated place, such as the minarets of old mosques or on the city's outskirts.

Issue 510: The criterion for the volume of the call to prayer is the average and customary volume. Regarding hearing the call to prayer, it is the average and normal hearing ability. Regarding weather conditions, it is the typical weather, meaning the weather without strong winds, dust, or fog.

Issue 511: If the traveler moves away until the call to prayer becomes inaudible, but other loud sounds, such as supplications and Qur'ānic recitations, are still audible, it is an obligatory precaution if he prays in that place to perform both qaṣr and tamām prayers, or he should move further until all sounds become inaudible.

Issue 512: If the traveler intends to stay in a place for ten days and has not reached ḥadd al-tarakhkhuṣ for that place, he should perform qaṣr prayers. As for the distance between this outer limit and the place of residence, it is an obligatory precaution to perform both qaṣr and tamām prayers.

Issue 513: If one leaves the place where he intended to stay for ten days, intending to cover the prescribed distance, it is an obligatory precaution to perform both qaṣr and tamām prayers in the distance between the place of residence and the outer limit or to delay the prayer until surpassing the outer limit and then perform qaṣr prayers.

Issue 514: If one stays in a place hesitantly for thirty days[32] and performs tamām prayers from the first to the thirtieth day, then leaves for the prescribed distance; it is an obligatory precaution to either perform both qaṣr and tamām prayers before reaching the outer limit or delay the prayer and perform qaṣr.

---

32 He does not know when he will leave that place, so he does not intend to stay for ten days.

Issue 515: In all other cases (except for the three specific cases)[33] where the traveler needed to perform tamām prayers and then his obligation shifted to qaṣr, the criterion for shortening the prayer here is not reaching the outer limit (ḥadd al-tarakhkhuṣ). An example is someone who initially intended an unlawful journey then changed it to permissible or who travels a distance of eight farsakhs without intending to travel and wishes to return.

Issue 516: If a traveler leaves his hometown aiming to cover the prescribed distance and is uncertain whether he has reached the outer limit or not, he must assume that he has not reached it and perform tamām prayers. If this uncertainty occurs on the return journey, he must perform qaṣr prayers. However, if he is uncertain in one place during both the outbound and return journeys regarding whether he has surpassed the outer limit and intends to pray there, he must perform both qaṣr and tamām prayers. If he performed tamām prayers only during the outbound journey, he must also repeat them as qaṣr prayers.

Issue 517: If one embarks on a journey from his hometown and performs qaṣr prayers before reaching the outer limit, working under the assumption that he has reached it, and then realizes his mistake, he must repeat the prayer. The same ruling applies if this occurs on the return journey and he performs tamām prayers.

---

[33] That is in all other cases except the following three: hometown, intention to stay ten days, and hesitancy for thirty days.

Issue 518: If one embarks on a journey from his hometown and prays tamām prayers after surpassing the outer limit, working under the assumption that he has not reached it, and then realizes his mistake, he must repeat the prayer. The same ruling applies if this occurs on the return journey and he performs qaṣr prayers.

Issue 519: If one leaves the hometown and surpasses the outer limit, then re-enters the outer limit again, he must perform tamām prayers inside the outer limit. There is no difference in whether his return is voluntary, involuntary, or due to deviation from the route.

Issue 520: In the scenario of the previous issue, if his entry into the outer limit is due to the nature of the route, such as in the event of a deviated route, then the remaining portion of the journey does not have to cover a prescribed distance. The prescribed distance is calculated from the journey's beginning, considering the distance traveled while entering and exiting the outer limit.

Issue 521: In the scenario of the previous issue, if entry into the outer limit is not due to a deviated route but for another optional or non-optional reason,[34] such as returning to retrieve a forgotten item within the outer limit, and after retrieving it, he returns to continue his journey on the same route. In this case, the prescribed distance is calculated from the beginning of the journey,

[34] Non-optional, such as a ship that sails towards a destination and leaves the outer limit, the winds push it back inside the outer limit.

but without considering the additional distance he traveled to return from outside the outer limit to retrieve the item and return to the same point.

Issue 522: If one surpasses the outer limit of the hometown aiming to cover the prescribed distance and performs qaṣr prayers, then returns within the outer limit, then resumes his journey again, what he already prayed suffices, and repetition is not required.

Issue 523: If one leaves the place where he intended to stay for ten days, intending to cover the prescribed distance, and after surpassing the outer limit, he returns within the outer limit or even to the place of residence for some reason and does not intend to stay for ten days, he should perform qaṣr prayers.

Issue 524: If a person intends to travel around the country for at least eight Farasikh, and his route is within the outer limit, he must perform tamām prayers. But if he is outside the outer limit, he should perform qaṣr prayers, even if he enters the outer sometimes due to deviation in the routes, and even if the distance outside the outer limit is less than eight Farasikh. However, if he intends to pray within the outer limit, he should perform tamām prayers.

Issue 525: In the scenario of the previous issue, if entry into the outer limit is not due to deviation in the route, but he chooses to return within the outer limit, then if the remaining portion of the journey—without considering the distance he covers to return to the outer limit and exit it—is less than eight Farasikh, he should perform tamām prayers. But if it [the remaining portion of the journey] is equal to the prescribed distance, then he should perform qaṣr prayers. However, if he intends to pray within the outer limit, he should perform tamām prayers.

Travel Interruptions

Issue 526: Travel is interrupted, and tamām prayers become obligatory in the following cases:

1. Passing through one's hometown.
2. Intending to stay in one place for at least ten days or knowing such intention.
3. Remaining hesitantly in one place for thirty days without intending to stay.

Passing through one's hometown:

Issue 527: If someone intends to travel a prescribed distance and his journey is interrupted by passing through his hometown, he must perform tamām prayers. If the remaining part of his journey to his destination is at least eight Farasikh (consecutive or non-consecutive), he should perform qaṣr prayers. If it is less than the prescribed distance, he should perform tamām prayers.

Issue 528: Merely passing through one's hometown (without stopping or staying) is sufficient to interrupt the travel.

Issue 529: The term "hometown" [waṭan] refers colloquially to the place where a person chooses to reside, settle, and make his living, whether it is a city, village, or any other place.

Issue 530: Hometowns are of two types: original and adopted.

Original Hometown:

Issue 531: The original hometown is where a person grew up and spent a significant part of his early life (childhood and adolescence).

Issue 532: It is not considered part of the original hometown merely because a person was born there or because it was his parents' hometown. Similarly, intending to live there permanently or for a long period does not necessarily make it the original hometown. Unless a person leaves it with the intention of not returning, the original hometown remains valid for him.

Issue 533: Determining the necessary time to establish the original hometown depends on custom ['urf]. For example, if someone spends the first ten years of his life in a place, it is considered his original hometown, according to 'urf.

However, if he stays there for only a year or two, it is not considered as such.

Adopted Hometown:

Issue 534: The adopted homeland, according to custom [ʿurf], is the place a person chooses as his hometown and residence, especially if it was not his original hometown, whether he has renounced[35] from his original hometown or not.

Issue 535: In establishing the adopted hometown, there is no distinction between intending permanent residency, indefinite residency, or long-term residency in that place.

Issue 536: If someone intends to stay in a place for around ten years, this duration is sufficient according to customary practice to establish the adopted hometown.

Issue 537: The mere intention is insufficient to establish the adopted hometown as per custom. Rather, it is necessary to fulfill residency requirements, such as staying there for a period (like a month or two) to take it as a hometown[36] and settle there or engaging in activities typically undertaken to settle in a particular place.

---

[35] Renouncing one's hometown here means that a person decides not to choose that land—his hometown—as a place for his residence ever again.

[36] That is, designating a place as one's waṭan (hometown).

Issue 538: If a person intends to settle in a place and rents or buys a house or starts a business or job from the outset, the hometown is established from that time, and one should perform tamām prayers there. The passage of a month or two is not considered necessary to establish it as the hometown.

Issue 539: If someone intends to settle in a place but hesitates to stay there before fulfilling the conditions for establishing residency (as mentioned in the preceding two issues), the hometown title is not established. If he does not intend to stay for ten days, he should perform qaṣr prayers.

Issue 540: If a person prepares a house in another city, like Mashhad ar-Riḍā ؑ, or in one of the summer tourism regions, and decides to visit it frequently, say every week, for Ziyārah or outings, if the duration of his stay in that place is not significant enough to be considered residency according to customary practice, he must perform qaṣr prayers there, and his fasting there is not valid.

Issue 541: The place a person chooses to live in for a year or two is not considered his hometown according to customary practice. However, it is not considered that he is traveling there either. Therefore, he should perform tamām prayers, even if he does not intend to stay for ten days.

Having Multiple Actual Hometowns

Issue 542: There is no problem if a person has two or three actual hometowns, each with a residence and living necessities, and he resides in each place for several months throughout the year. However, having more than three actual homelands is questionable.

Issue 543: If someone intends to live permanently or for several years for a period of three or four months each year (such as during the summer or vacation days), and he prepares the necessities of living, such as the house and the like, then that place is considered, by customary practice, a second hometown for him. However, establishing it as a hometown is unlikely if he only goes on vacation without intending to settle down and without preparing living necessities there.

Issue 544: Establishing a hometown is not considered for someone who lives in multiple places if he does not spend equal periods in each place. For example, if someone has two hometowns and spends five months in one and seven months in the other, or if someone has three hometowns and spends four months in one, five months in another, and three months in the third, then the ruling of hometown applies to all of them.

Hometown Affiliation:

Issue 545: Affiliation in hometown is a matter of custom [ʿurf] just like the hometown itself, meaning that a child who lives with his parents, or with one of them, is considered by custom to be affiliated with them, and their hometown is also considered his hometown.

Issue 546: Affiliation in hometown occurs in the adopted hometown rather than the original hometown. For example, suppose a person grows up and spends their childhood and adolescence in a certain place. That place is considered his original hometown, whether it is his parents' hometown or not.

Issue 547: An original hometown is established if a child does not live in his parents' hometown (the original or the adopted hometown) for a period. For instance, if a child moves away from his parents for some reason after birth and grows up elsewhere, then returns to live with them after, let us say, ten years, in this case, his parents' hometown is no longer considered his original hometown. Instead, upon returning, the place becomes an adopted hometown for the child based on his residence with his parents.

Issue 548: Affiliation in hometown is not limited to children but also includes, according to custom, anyone who follows another person, such as a servant hired to accompany someone permanently or a wife who does not stipulate living in a specific place and lives with her husband permanently.

Issue 549: In establishing hometown affiliation, the follower does not need to intend to settle down; merely accompanying the one followed suffices, even if unintentional, provided there is no intention of renunciation or refusal to settle down.

Issue 550: In the case of a child who has reached puberty, such as a girl at the age of eleven or twelve or a boy at the age of sixteen or seventeen, if they accompany their parents to a country intending to settle down, even if the child is unaware of the intention to settle, that place also becomes their hometown.

Issue 551: If a child accompanies his parents to a place intending to settle down [make it their hometown], but the child intends not to settle, then that place is not considered his hometown, even if he is in their care.

Issue 552: If a child who intended to settle in a place following his parents changes his mind after a period (for example, a month or two), as long as he did not leave that place, his change of intention is not realized, and he must perform tamām prayers.

Renouncing One's Hometown:

Issue 553: Renouncing one's hometown (like establishing it) is a matter of custom ['urf], meaning that a person leaves his hometown to avoid returning to reside there.

Issue 554: Whoever renounces his hometown (whether it is the original or adopted one), whenever he intends to go there, he must perform qaṣr prayers, whether he has property there or not. Passing through that place is not an interrupter of travel unless he intends to stay for ten days.

Issue 555: Intent and purpose are considered when renouncing one's hometown. If someone leaves the hometown without intending to renounce it, for four or five years, for example, without intending to renounce, that place remains his hometown. However, if he leaves his hometown for a very long period, such as forty or fifty years, and does not consider returning throughout this period, then in this case, it is not far-fetched to consider the absence as renunciation, and he must perform qaṣr prayers there if he does not intend to stay for ten days.

Issue 556: If someone leaves his hometown without making the intention of not returning but knows or is certain that he will not return[37] to live there, this knowledge and certainty may also be considered renunciation. He must thus perform qaṣr prayers there.

Issue 557: A wife who lives in a place other than her original hometown following her husband and did not intend to renounce her hometown if she does not have knowledge or assurance that she will never return to her hometown until the end of her life, but rather, even as a result of a specific event such as separation from her husband or his death, then she must perform tamām prayers there. However, if her decision is not to return even after her husband's death or separation from him, then in this case, renunciation is established. That place is not considered her hometown anymore.

Intention to Stay for Ten Days:

Issue 558: If a traveler intends to stay in a place for ten days, he should perform tamām prayers there. However, if he

---

[37] Regarding the one who leaves his hometown, there are three scenarios:

a. If he intends to return or knows that he will return, his hometown remains as such.
b. If he intends not to return or knows he will not return, renunciation of his hometown is realized.
c. If he has not decided on his return or non-return and has no knowledge, his hometown remains as is unless forty or fifty years have passed. The thought of returning there has not crossed his mind during this period.

remains in one place for ten days without intention or hesitation, he should perform qaṣr prayers.

Issue 559: If a person does not intend to stay for ten days but is certain or assured that he will stay in one place for ten days, he should perform tamām prayers. However, if he only suspects he will stay, he should perform qaṣr prayers.

Issue 560: The ten days of stay must be consecutive and continuous, and one should not intend to embark on a journey that necessitates performing qaṣr prayers during that time. If he intends to stay in a place for five days, then travels for ten Farasikh afterward and returns, then stay for another five days, the intention of staying is not fulfilled, and he should perform qaṣr prayers from the beginning.

Issue 561: If, during the intention of staying, a person plans to leave his location for less than four Farasikh,[38] suppose the intention is to leave within a time frame that does not negate the customary stay of ten days, such as intending to leave two or three times during this period, not exceeding half a day each time at maximum. In that case, the intention of staying is not invalidated, and he should perform tamām prayers.

Issue 562: "Day" in the context of a ten-day stay refers to the customary definition: from sunrise to sunset. Therefore, if a person arrives at a place at sunrise and

---

[38] This means that intending to travel a distance shorter than the prescribed distance is comparable to intending to stay for ten days.

intends to stay until the sunset of the tenth day, he should perform tamām prayers, and he does not need to be there during the first and last nights.

Issue 563: In the intention of a ten-day stay, the intermediate nights are also considered part of the ten days. Therefore, a person who intends to stay in a place cannot leave it at night by a distance equal to the distance prescribed by Islāmic law.

Issue 564: If a traveler intends to stay for less than ten days (even by just an hour), it is not sufficient to fulfill the intention of staying, and he should thus perform qaṣr prayers.

Issue 565: Whoever intends to stay for ten days should continue performing tamām prayers after completing the ten days as long as he is still in that place and has not left. He does not need to make a new intention to stay.

Issue 566: If a person arrives at a place after sunrise intending to stay there for ten days, he must spend the same amount of time after sunrise on the eleventh day as he spent after sunrise when he arrived at the place to complete the ten days. For example, if he arrived on the first day at a place three hours after sunrise and intended to stay until three hours after sunrise on the eleventh day, he should perform tamām prayers.

Issue 567: The place of stay for the ten days must be considered one place according to custom [ʿurf], and a mere connection between two places (such as two cities or villages) is not sufficient unless they are considered one place according to custom.

Issue 568: If the city where he intends to stay is one of the major cities consisting of interconnected neighborhoods, his intention to move between its neighborhoods does not affect the unity of the place of stay.

Issue 569: In case of doubt about the unity of the place of stay, he should perform qaṣr prayers.

Issue 570: If his intention to stay in a place is conditional upon realizing a doubtful or suspected event, his intention to stay is not fulfilled, and he should perform qaṣr prayers. This is similar to someone whose stay is contingent upon the arrival of a person, not knowing whether they will come or even suspecting their arrival.

Issue 571: If he intends to stay for ten days but there is a possibility of an obstacle preventing him from staying for the full ten days, and if this possibility is weak and not a concern for sensible people, his intention to stay is fulfilled, and he must perform tamām prayers. However, if the possibility is strong and sensible people consider it, his intention to stay is not fulfilled, and he must perform qaṣr prayers.

Issue 572: If he intends to stay in a place until a specific day (such as the end of the month) but the actual duration is ten days, the intention of staying is fulfilled even if he did not know it was ten days, and he should perform tamām prayers. Although, it is recommended to perform both qaṣr and tamām prayers in such a case.

Issue 573: If he intends to stay in a place until a specific day, such as Monday (and no more), and he intends to stay for ten days believing that the duration until that time is ten days (although it is less than that), his prayer, in this case, is qaṣr. If he realizes his miscalculation during the time of the prayer, he must repeat the prayer. Otherwise, if the time for the prayer has passed, then it is an obligatory precaution that he makes it up.

Issue 574: If someone intends to stay for ten days in a specific place and imagines that the ten days will be completed on a certain day (although it is less than ten days), but he intended that if the period until that day is less than ten days, he will certainly stay for additional days to complete the ten days, then in this case, he should perform tamām prayers.

Issue 575: Performing the prayer is not a condition for fulfilling the intention to stay. Therefore, if a menstruating or postpartum woman intends to stay for ten days, her intention is valid, and the days she does not pray are counted as part of the ten days.

Issue 576: If a traveler intends to stay for ten days while performing qaṣr prayers, he must complete the prayer as tamām with four units.

Changing One's Mind About the Intention to Stay:

Issue 577: If the traveler who intended to stay for ten days changes his intention or hesitates in this regard before performing a four-unit obligatory prayer, he should perform qaṣr prayers.

Issue 578: If someone intends to stay for ten days and performs a four-unit obligatory prayer in fulfillment of duty [adā'], he should keep the prayer tamām as long as he remains in that place, even if he changes his intention and decides not to stay for ten days anymore. However, if he only prayed Fajr or Maghrib and then changed his intention, he should perform qaṣr prayers.

Issue 579: If someone changes his mind about staying for ten days while performing the first unit of a four-unit obligatory prayer and decides to stay for less than ten days, he should revert to performing qaṣr prayers. If he changes his mind before entering the third unit, he should continue the prayer as qaṣr. But if he changes his mind after entering the third unit but before bowing, then it is an obligatory precaution for him to sit and continue his prayer as qaṣr, and then he should also repeat it as qaṣr. However, if he has already begun with the bowing of the third unit, then his prayer is invalid.

Issue 580: If someone intends to stay for ten days and then intends to fast but changes his intention before performing a four-unit obligatory prayer, his fast is valid if his intention changes after midday. However, if it happens before midday, his fast is invalid.

Issue 581: If someone misses a four-unit obligatory prayer after intending to stay for ten days and then changes his intention without performing another four-unit obligatory prayer in fulfillment of duty [adā'] (not lapsed), he should perform the subsequent prayers as qaṣr. However, the missed prayer must be made up as tamām even during travel.

Issue 582: In the previous issue, if someone had made up the missed prayer as tamām during the same journey and then changed his intention about staying for ten days, he should perform qaṣr prayers. And his lapsed four-unit obligatory prayer does not suffice to make his subsequent prayers tamām.

Issue 583: If someone changes his intention after performing a four-unit obligatory prayer and then realizes that his prayer is invalid, his duty is to perform qaṣr prayers.

Issue 584: If someone changes his intention after the time for the four-unit obligatory prayer has passed and doubts whether he prayed before the time ended, he must assume that he performed the prayer as tamām and continue to pray subsequent prayers as tamām accordingly.

Issue 585: If someone doubts after changing his intention whether he prayed a four-unit obligatory prayer before changing his intention or not, he should perform qaṣr prayers.

Leaving the Place of Stay:

Issue 586: If someone wishes, after realizing the intention to stay, to leave his place of stay to cover a distance of less than four Farasikh (even for a day or more), there is no problem with that, and it does not harm the intention of staying.

Issue 587: If someone decides, after realizing the intention to stay, to head (whether within the initial ten days or afterward) to a destination less than four Farasikh away, with the intention of returning to the place of stay (considering it as the place of stay), he should perform tamām prayers on the way there and back, as well as at the destination and the place of stay.

Staying a Month in a Place Without Intending to Stay:

Issue 588: If someone stays in a single location for thirty days hesitatingly, after traveling eight Farasikh, he should perform tamām prayers after the thirtieth day as long as he has not left that place (even if it is for half a day).

Issue 589: A traveler who intended to stay in a single location for less than ten days, if he changes his mind about leaving after the specified period and then decides again to stay for less than ten days (for example, a week), then extends his stay in the same manner until a month elapses, acts as described in the previous issue: he should perform tamām prayers on the thirty-first day and onwards.

Issue 590: If someone stays in a single location hesitatingly for less than thirty days (for example, twenty-eight days), then goes to another place and stays there hesitatingly for less than thirty days as well, and similarly in a third place, he should perform qaṣr prayers in all three places.

Issue 591: The thirty days are calculated as follows: If someone arrives at a place at sunrise, he should perform tamām prayers after sunset on the thirtieth day, meaning he prays the 'Ishā' prayer of the thirtieth day and the subsequent obligatory prayers as tamām. If he arrives after sunrise, the thirty days are completed at the same hour of his arrival on the thirty-first day. For example, if he arrives an hour after sunrise, the thirty days are completed an hour after sunrise on the thirty-first day, and he should perform the obligatory four-unit prayers as tamām after that.

Issue 592: If the lunar month consists of twenty-nine days, he should perform qaṣr prayers until the twenty-ninth day, and on the thirtieth day (the first day of the next month), he should perform both qaṣr and tamām prayers based on obligatory precaution. Then, he should perform tamām prayers on the thirty-first day and afterward.

Issue 593: It is a condition for the place where one expresses hesitation (regarding the intention to stay) to be recognized as one place by custom [ʿurf]. For instance, if someone spends part of the thirty days in one recognized location, like Tehrān, and another part in another city, like Karaj,[39] then the ruling of hesitation for thirty days does not apply in this case, and he should continue performing qaṣr prayers.

Issue 594: If someone leaves during the period of hesitation to a place less than four Farasikh away, and if his leaving does not conflict with the recognized period of staying for thirty days in one location and does not harm it, he should perform tamām prayers after the completion of the thirty days. The same applies if he leaves for part of the day (not the entire day) and his leaving is not frequent, such as leaving and returning four or five times during the thirty days, spending three or four hours each.

Issue 595: If someone stays in a location for thirty days without intending to stay, then from the thirty-first day, it is considered as if he intended to stay, so he must perform tamām prayers after completing the thirtieth day. If he intends to head out for a distance less than the prescribed distance prescribed by Islāmic law [for shortening prayers], the same rulings mentioned in the section on staying for ten days apply in this case. For example, suppose he intends to go to a place less than four Farasikh away and return to

---

[39] Karaj is a city close to Tehrān.

his place of stay for thirty days, where he resides without intending to stay. In that case, he should perform tamām prayers on the way there and back, at the destination and where he returned.

Issue 596: If someone's duty is to perform tamām prayers after staying in one place for thirty days, and then he leaves that place intending to travel as per Islāmic law [covering the prescribed distance], it is obligatory precaution that he either perform both qaṣr and tamām prayers in the distance between the place of stay for thirty days and the starting point of the journey or delay his prayers and then perform them as qaṣr.

Ruling of the Recommended Prayers During Travel

Issue 597: It is not permissible to perform the recommended prayers [nawāfil] of Ẓuhr and 'Aṣr during travel in which prayers are shortened (even with the intention of hoping for its acceptance and reward [rajā']).

Issue 598: There is no problem in performing the recommended prayer of 'Ishā' (the Watīrah prayer) during travel with the intention of hoping for its acceptance and reward.

Issue 599: The recommended prayers [nawāfil] that become void for a traveler are allowed and recommended [mustaḥabb] for those who intend to stay for ten days, and the recommended fasting is also recommended for them.

Issue 600: If the accountable person [mukallaf] intends to perform tamām prayers in places where he can choose between either qaṣr or tamām prayers, he can also perform the recommended daily prayers.

Issue 601: The recommended night prayer and the nawāfil of Fajr and Maghrib are not void for travelers.

Issue 602: The recommended prayers other than the daily nawāfil prayers, such as the Ja'far aṭ-Ṭayyār prayer (which is a very important prayer and holds significant merit), the prayer of the Imām of Time, and the prayers specific to certain days such as Friday prayers, do not become void for a traveler.

Ruling of Performing Tamām Prayer When Qaṣr Prayer is Obligatory

Issue 603: If a traveler knows that it is obligatory to shorten prayers during travel when its conditions are met, and he also knows that his journey fulfills those conditions, but he still performs tamām prayers, his prayers are invalid, and he must repeat them shortened, whether it is within the prayer time or outside it.

Issue 604: If a traveler does not know that shortening prayers is obligatory during travel, and he performs tamām prayers contrary to his duty if he is an inculpable ignorant,[40] then he is excused, and there is no obligation to repeat or make up the prayer after learning the ruling.

Issue 605: In the scenario of the previous issue, if the person is a culpable ignorant,[41] then he disobeyed due to his negligence in learning the ruling, and after learning the ruling, he must repeat the prayer within its time and make it up if the time has already passed.

Issue 606: If someone knows the ruling of shortening prayers during travel but performs tamām prayers due to ignorance about the specifics of the ruling, in this case, it is an obligatory precaution for him to repeat the prayer if he realizes that within the prayer time and to make it up if he realizes that after its time has passed. This also applies if he knew that prayers during travel should be shortened. However, he still performed them as tamām due to ignorance that his duty was to perform the prayers as qaṣr if he intended to stay for ten days. He then changed his intention before performing a four-unit obligatory prayer.

Issue 607: If a traveler knows the ruling of shortening prayers during travel but performs tamām prayers because he is ignorant that he is in a state of travel as prescribed by Islāmic law, he must repeat the prayer. For example, if he

---

[40] An inculpable ignorant [jāhil qāṣir] is unaware of his ignorance or knows of his ignorance but cannot find a way out of it.

[41] A culpable ignorant [jāhil muqaṣṣir] is aware of his ignorance and knows of it but is negligent in learning the rulings.

knows that the traveler must shorten the prayer and intends to travel to a place eight Farasikh away but mistakenly believes the distance to be seven Farasikh, he performs tamām prayers. However, his actual duty is to perform qaṣr prayers.

Issue 608: If someone forgets that the traveler must perform qaṣr prayers or forgets that he is a traveler and performs tamām prayers, if he remembers within the prayer time, he must repeat the prayer. If he does not remember within the time, there is no obligation to make it up. If he realizes this outside the prayer time, there is no obligation to make it up.

Issue 609: If a traveler does not know that he must perform qaṣr prayers if he misses the prayer and then realizes the ruling after the prayer time has ended, he must make up the missed prayer as qaṣr.

Issue 610: In the scenario of the previous issue, if he performs the missed prayer[42] as tamām and then realizes the ruling, if he is an inculpable ignorant, he is not obligated to repeat it as qaṣr.

Issue 611: If someone forgets that the traveler must perform the prayer as qaṣr or forgets that he is a traveler and begins the prayer intending to perform it as tamām, and he remembers before standing for the third unit of prayer, he

[42] The obligatory prayer that he did not perform at its specific time.

should complete his prayer with the two units, and it is valid in this way. If he remembers after standing for the third unit but before bowing, he must sit back down and end the prayer with a salutation.

Issue 612: In the scenario of the previous issue, if he remembers after entering the bowing position of the third unit, his prayer is invalid, whether there is still ample time or not enough, even if there is not enough time left for one single unit of prayer, and he must repeat or make it up.

Ruling of Qaṣr Prayer When Tamām Prayer is Obligatory

Issue 613: If a traveler whose duty is to perform tamām prayers performs qaṣr prayers instead contrary to his duty, his prayer is invalid. There is no difference in this ruling whether the action was done knowingly, intentionally, due to forgetfulness, or out of ignorance of the ruling or the matter [e.g., his situation, circumstances that warrant this ruling], except in the specific case that will be mentioned in the subsequent issue.

Issue 614: If a traveler who intends to stay for ten days in a place performs qaṣr prayers due to ignorance of the ruling, his prayer is valid. However, if the shortening was due to ignorance of the matter [e.g., his situation and circumstances that warrant this ruling] or forgetfulness, his prayer is invalid, and he must repeat it.

Issue 615: If someone whose duty is to perform tamām prayers, such as a traveler intending to stay for ten days, begins the prayer with the intention of qaṣr due to forgetfulness or ignorance of the ruling or matter [e.g., his situation, circumstances, that warrant this ruling], and he realizes that before starting with the salutation [taslīm],[43] which concludes the prayer; he should complete his prayer as tamām, and it will be valid.

Miscellaneous Issues

Issue 616: If a person, at the prime time of prayer and while in his hometown or the place where he intends to stay for ten days, travels without performing the prayer, then if he wishes to pray while traveling, he should perform it as qaṣr.

Issue 617: If a traveler does not pray during the prime time of prayer and then arrives back in his hometown or the place of intended residence, he should perform the prayer as tamām.

Issue 618: If a traveler does not pray during the prime time of prayer after he reaches his hometown or the place of

---

[43] The first taslīm—which is "As-salāmu ʿalayka ayyuhā an-nabiyyū wa-raḥmatu Allāhi wa-barakātuhū"—is a recommended [mustaḥabbb] taslīm, and thus it is not considered that one has finished prayer with it. Reciting the second taslīm—"As-salāmu ʿalaynā wa ʿalā ʿibādillāhiṣ ṣāliḥīn"—or the third taslīm—"As-salāmu ʿalaykum wa raḥmatullāhi wa barakātuh"—necessitate that one has finished the prayer.

intended residence and the time for the prayer has passed, he must make up for it as tamām.

Issue 619: If a person was during the prime time of a prayer in his hometown or the place of intended residence, and then he travels and misses the prayer in his journey, he must make up for it as qaṣr.

Issue 620: At Makkah, Madīnah (Medina), Kūfah Mosque, and the shrine of Imām al-Ḥusayn, a traveler may choose between performing qaṣr or tamām prayers for obligatory four-unit prayers, with tamām prayers being preferable, although qaṣr prayers are the recommended precaution.

Issue 621: The ruling of choice between qaṣr and tamām prayers applies to the entire cities of Makkah and Madīnah, not just limited to the Sacred Mosque [Masjid al-Ḥarām] and the Prophet's Mosque. However, it is recommended precaution to confine oneself to these mosques [concerning the ruling].

Issue 622: In Kūfah, the ruling of choice applies specifically to the Kūfah Mosque, and based on obligatory precaution, this ruling does not apply to the entire city of Kūfah.

Issue 623: In the shrine of Imām al-Ḥusayn, the ruling of choice is limited to the area beneath the dome and the place identified as the grave of Imām al-Ḥusayn 🏵, not including the corridors and the purified courtyard based on obligatory precaution.

Issue 624: The ruling of choice between qaṣr and tamām prayers in the aforementioned sacred places is continuous, allowing the traveler to perform whichever obligatory four-unit prayers he wishes as tamām and whichever of them he wishes as qaṣr.

Issue 625: If the accountable person misses a prayer (intentionally or inadvertently) in these four places where the ruling of choice applies, and he intends to make them up elsewhere, it is stronger to make up for them as qaṣr. Even if he intends to make up for them in these four places, it is an obligatory precaution to make up for them as qaṣr.

Issue 626: The ruling of choice between qaṣr and tamām prayers in the aforementioned four places does not apply to fasting. Therefore, a traveler cannot fast during the month of Ramaḍān in these places.

Lapsed [Qaḍā'] Prayer

Issue 627: If someone intentionally, forgetfully, or out of ignorance does not perform the obligatory daily prayer within its prescribed time or realizes after the time has passed that his prayer is invalid, he must make it up [perform it as qaḍā'].

Issue 628: If someone fails to perform a non-daily obligatory prayer, such as the Prayer of Signs [Ṣalāt al-Āyāt], within its designated time, he must make it up.

Issue 629: The obligation to make up missed prayers arises only when the Islāmically accountable person [mukallaf] is certain that he neglected it or that his prayer was invalid. If he is doubtful or suspicious about either neglecting it or it being invalid, there is no obligation to make it up.

Issue 630: If a responsible person is in a state of unconsciousness during the entire prayer time, he is not obligated to make it up unless the unconsciousness was caused by his action, in which case making it up becomes obligatory based on obligatory precaution.

Issue 631: A non-Muslim who embraces Islām is not obligated to make up the missed prayers before his conversion to Islām. However, an apostate—someone who renounced Islām—must, after repentance, make up for prayers missed during his apostasy.

Issue 632: It is not obligatory to make up prayers at the time of which the woman was menstruating or experiencing postpartum bleeding.

Issue 633: It is not obligatory to immediately make up for missed prayers, but negligence and leniency are not permissible.

Issue 634: If someone prays without ritual purity from a certain impurity [ḥadath; those impurities which require intention for cleaning, like those things after which ablution or ghusl becomes necessary] out of ignorance of the matter or the religious ruling, such as someone unaware that he is in a state of major ritual impurity [janābah] and does not perform the required major ablution [ghusl], he must make up the prayer.

Issue 635: Obligatory prayers must be made up exactly as they were missed. If it was the individual's duty to perform a tamām prayer and he missed it, he must make it up as tamām even during travel. Similarly, if he missed four-unit prayers during travel (where his duty was to shorten the prayer), he must make them up as qaṣr even if he is not traveling.

Issue 636: Obligatory prayers can be made up at any time of the day or night. It is not obligatory to make up the Fajr prayer, for example, at the time of Fajr, and make up the Ẓuhr prayer at the time of Ẓuhr.

Issue 637: The criterion for making up missed prayers is the end of their times. If a person is traveling at the end of the prayer time, he must make it up as qaṣr, even if he was in his hometown during the prime time of the prayer. However, if he is not traveling at the end of the prayer time, he must make it up as tamām, even if he was traveling during the prime time of the prayer.

Issue 638: There is no obligation to observe the sequence between qaḍā' prayers, except in making up Ẓuhr and 'Aṣr prayers from the same day and making up Maghrib and 'Ishā' prayers from the same day.

Issue 639: If someone does not know the number of his missed prayers, he may suffice with the best estimation of their number.

Issue 640: Making up missed prayers must be prioritized over performing current prayers. However, based on obligatory precaution, someone with only one missed prayer should make it up first, especially if it is missed on that same day.

Issue 641: It is permissible for someone with make-up prayers to perform the nawāfil and recommended prayers.

Issue 642: It is recommended [mustaḥabb] to make up the daily nawāfil.

Hired Prayers

Issue 643: If a deceased person has missed acts of worship such as prayers and fasting, hiring someone to perform them on his behalf is permissible. It is also permissible to volunteer[44] to make them up on his behalf, thus fulfilling the deceased's responsibility.

Issue 644: The prayer performed on behalf of the deceased in return for a fee is termed "hired prayers" [Ṣalāt al-Isti'jāriyyah].

---

[44] Making up for free without awaiting anything in return.

Issue 645: If the deceased has specified hiring someone to make up his missed prayers in his will, one-third of his estate must be allocated for that purpose. Any amount exceeding one-third requires the permission of the heirs.

Issue 646: If someone is hired to make up prayers for a deceased person, specifying the deceased and their particulars is unnecessary. It suffices to identify them in a general and whole manner. For example, if someone is hired to perform prayers for two individuals, intending the prayer for the deceased who was hired first is sufficient.

Issue 647: If the one hiring does not specify any particular conditions (such as praying in the congregation or at the mosque), then the obligation of the hired person is limited to performing the prayers with their obligatory components only.

Issue 648: In hired prayers, it is not a condition for the hired person to be of the same gender as the deceased. It is permissible for a man to make up prayers for a woman, and vice versa, whether they are hired or volunteers.

Issue 649: The hired person must work according to his or her duty when performing the prayers aloud or in a whisper. For example, if a man is hired to make up the prayers of a woman, then he must recite Sūrat al-Fātiḥah and the other Sūrah aloud in the Fajr, Maghrib, and 'Ishā' prayers (as is the man's obligation in prayer).

Issue 650: The person making up prayers on behalf of the deceased must fulfill certain conditions:

1. Knowledge of the rules and regulations of prayer based on either personal reasoning [ijtihād] or valid emulation [of a marjaʿ].

2. Assurance in performing the prayer correctly.

3. Not being one of those who have valid excuses. For instance, someone who prays sitting cannot be hired to make up prayers for the deceased.

Making Up the Prayers of Parents

Issue 651: The eldest son is obliged to make up the missed prayers of his father, and it is an obligatory precaution for him to make them up on behalf of his mother as well.

Issue 652: If the father or mother completely neglects prayer, the eldest son is obliged to make up their prayers on their behalf as a precaution.

Issue 653: The eldest son refers to the eldest male child who is alive at the time of the death of the father and mother, whether he has reached puberty or not.

Issue 654: If the eldest child of the deceased is a daughter and the second child is a son, then the elder son (i.e., the second child) is obliged to make up the missed prayers of the father, as well as the missed prayers of the mother as a precaution.

Issue 655: If someone else (other than the eldest son) makes up the parents' prayers, then the eldest son's obligation is lifted.

Issue 656: The eldest son must make up the confirmed number of missed prayers on behalf of his parents. If he is unaware of any missed prayers, there is no obligation or requirement for investigation or inquiry.

Issue 657: The eldest son is obliged to make up the prayers of his parents in any possible way. If he cannot do so, there is no obligation upon him.

Issue 658: If someone must make up prayers for himself and his parents, he may choose which to prioritize. He can focus on making up whichever set of prayers he prefers first.

Issue 659: If the eldest son dies after the death of his father and mother, there is no obligation for the prayers of the parents to be made up by any of the other children.

Ṣalāt al-Āyāt [Prayer of the Signs]

Some natural phenomena, such as earthquakes, solar eclipses, lunar eclipses, terrifying storms, thunder, and lightning, are signs that always remind humans of the Day of Judgment and the greatness and power of God. During these times, turning to God, who is the source of all power, and performing the two units of Ṣalāt al-Āyāt [Prayer of the Signs] transforms one's state of fear, anxiety and worry into peace and tranquility, reminds him of God's ﷻ providence and system in His creation, and strengthens the spirit of monotheism against inclinations towards superstitions. Performing these two units of prayer is a means to shift the human mind from focusing on the "phenomenon" to the "Creator of the phenomenon."

Issue 660: Ṣalāt al-Āyāt becomes obligatory when one of the following four events occurs:

1. Solar eclipse, even if only partial, no matter how small the occurrence.

2. Lunar eclipse, even if only partial, no matter how small the occurrence.

3. Earthquake.

4. Any celestial event that frightens most people, such as black or red winds or lightning.

Issue 661: Ṣalāt al-Āyāt is not obligatory—except for during eclipses and earthquakes, where it is obligatory—unless the event is frightening to most people. If it is not frightening or only feared by some people, the prayer is not obligatory.

Issue 662: If the cause warranting the obligation of Ṣalāt al-Āyāt recurs more than once, the prayer becomes obligatory for each occurrence separately.

Issue 663: Ṣalāt al-Āyāt becomes obligatory for every earthquake, whether severe or mild, even for aftershocks if they are considered independent earthquakes.

Issue 664: The obligation of Ṣalāt al-Āyāt applies to individuals present at the location of the event during its occurrence.

Issue 665: The occurrences that necessitate the obligation of Ṣalāt al-Āyāt are established and confirmed by one of the following three methods:

1. Feeling the event personally.
2. Through any means that provide knowledge or assurance.
3. Testimony from two just witnesses.

Timing of Ṣalāt al-Āyāt

Issue 666: The time for the obligation of Ṣalāt al-Āyāt during solar and lunar eclipses starts when the disk begins to burn, and it is an obligatory precaution not to delay it until the stage of "ingression" begins.

Issue 667: If the accountable person delays Ṣalāt al-Āyāt until the sun or moon begins to ingress, then it becomes obligatory for him to perform the prayer to seek nearness to God without the intention of fulfilling the duty [adā'] or making up [qaḍā'] (to fulfill what is due), and if he delays it until the completion of the ingression, then it becomes obligatory for him to perform it to make up [qaḍā'].

Issue 668: When an earthquake or thunder and lightning, or similar events (which last for a short period) occur, it is obligatory precaution to perform Ṣalāt al-Āyāt immediately. If one delays, he is obligated to perform it until the end of his life without the intention of fulfilling the duty [adā'] or making up [qaḍā'] (with the intention of fulfilling what is due).

Issue 669: If a seismic monitoring center in a specific area announces the occurrence of minor earthquakes that are only detectable through devices and are not felt by the people living in that area, then Ṣalāt al-Āyāt is not obligatory.

Issue 670: If someone is unaware of a solar or lunar eclipse until the ingression stage is complete, and the disk burns completely, then it becomes obligatory for him to make up Ṣalāt al-Āyāt as qaḍā'. However, if only a part of the disk burns, then making it up is not obligatory.

Issue 671: If someone knows about the solar or lunar eclipse at their respective times and fails to perform Ṣalāt al-

Āyāt (even due to forgetfulness), then it becomes obligatory for him to make it up as qaḍā', even if the entire disk did not burn.

Issue 672: If someone becomes aware of an event (other than solar or lunar eclipse) at its time and fails to perform Ṣalāt al-Āyāt (even due to forgetfulness), then it becomes obligatory for him to perform it. However, if he becomes aware of the event after its occurrence, it is an obligatory precaution for him to perform its prayer.

Method of Performing Ṣalāt al-Āyāt

Issue 673: Ṣalāt al-Āyāt consists of two units, each of which includes five bowings [rukū'] and two prostrations [sujūd]. It can be performed in several ways:

1. First method: In each unit, one recites Sūrat al-Fātiḥah and another full Sūrah five times. After the intention and Takbīrat al-Iḥrām, one recites Sūrat al-Fātiḥah and another full Sūrah, then bows, then raises his head from bowing and recites Sūrat al-Fātiḥah and another full Sūrah, then bows for the second time, then raises his head from bowing, and so on for five bowings. After the fifth bowing, one prostrates twice, then rises to perform the second unit like the first. After the two prostrations, one recites tashahhud and taslīm.

2. Second method: In the first unit, one recites Sūrat al-Fātiḥah and another Sūrah once, dividing the Sūrah

into five parts; after the intention and Takbīrat al-Iḥrām, one recites Sūrat al-Fātiḥah and a part of the Sūrah (a verse or more or less), then bows. After rising from bowing, one recites only another part of the Sūrah without reciting Sūrat al-Fātiḥah and continues in this manner until the last part of the Sūrah, which is recited before the fifth bowing. After the fifth bowing, one prostrates twice, then rises to perform the second unit like the first. After the two prostrations, one recites tashahhud and taslīm.

Issue 674: It is an obligatory precaution not to divide the phrase "bismil lāhir raḥmānir raḥīm" [in the name of God, the Beneficent, the Merciful] as part of the Sūrah, and bowing afterward.

Issue 675: Whatever is obligatory or recommended in the daily obligatory prayers has the same ruling in Ṣalāt al-Āyāt. However, instead of the Adhān and Iqāmah, one says "Aṣṣalātu" [Prayer] three times, hoping for the reward.

Issue 676: It is recommended to say "samiʿal lāhu liman ḥamidah" [God hears the one who praises Him] after the fifth and tenth bowings. Also, saying takbīr before and after each bowing is recommended, but saying takbīr after the fifth and tenth bowings is not recommended.

Issue 677: It is recommended to perform Qunūt before the second, fourth, sixth, eighth, and tenth bowings, and it is sufficient to perform Qunūt only once before the tenth bowing.

Doubt in Ṣalāt al-Āyāt

Issue 678: If the praying person doubts between the fourth and fifth bowings, which occurs before the bending for prostration, it is obligatory to perform another bowing. However, if a doubt occurs after that, one should dismiss it.

Issue 679: Each of the bowings in Ṣalāt al-Āyāt is a pillar [rukn], and the prayer is invalidated by intentionally or inadvertently increasing or decreasing the number of bowings.

Issue 680: If one becomes aware that the Ṣalāt al-Āyāt which he has performed is invalid, then it is obligatory to repeat it if it is still within the time for it and to make up for it if its time has passed.

Prayers of ʿĪd al-Fiṭr and ʿĪd al-Aḍḥa

Issue 681: Performing the ʿĪd prayers for ʿĪd al-Fiṭr and ʿĪd al-Aḍḥa is obligatory during the presence of the infallible عليه السلام, and it is obligatory to establish them in the congregation. However, in the present era (the time of the major occultation), it is recommended [mustaḥabb].

Issue 682: The ʿĪd prayers for ʿĪd al-Fiṭr and ʿĪd al-Aḍḥa are from sunrise on the day of ʿĪd until noon.

Issue 683: It is recommended to establish the ʿĪd prayer for ʿĪd al-Aḍḥa after the sun has risen, whereas for ʿĪd al-Fiṭr, after the sun has risen, it is recommended for people to break their fast and give Zakāt al-Fiṭr first, then establish the ʿĪd prayer.

Issue 684: The ʿĪd prayers for ʿĪd al-Fiṭr and ʿĪd al-Aḍḥa consist of two units. In the first unit, after the recitation of Sūrat al-Fātiḥah and a Sūrah, five takbīrs are performed. After each takbīr, Qunūt is made, then another takbīr is made after the fifth Qunūt, followed by bowing. Then, after the two prostrations, one rises for the second unit, recites Sūrat al-Fātiḥah and another Sūrah, and performs four takbīrs. After each takbīr, Qunūt is made, then the fifth takbīr is said, followed by bowing, and the prayer is completed.

Issue 685: It is recommended to recite aloud during the ʿĪd prayers for ʿĪd al-Fiṭr and ʿĪd al-Aḍḥa.

Issue 686: Reciting specific Sūrahs in the ʿĪd prayers is unnecessary. However, it is preferable to recite Sūrat ash-Shams in the first unit and Sūrat al-Ghāshiyah in the second unit or Sūrat al-Aʿlā in the first unit and Sūrat ash-Shams in the second unit.

Issue 687: It is permissible to recite all kinds of remembrances and supplications during the Qunūt of the prayers of ʿĪd al-Fiṭr and ʿĪd al-Aḍḥa. However, it is preferable to recite the following supplication with the hope of gaining reward:

Transliteration: "Allāhumma ahlal kibriyāʾi wal ʿaẓamah, wa ahlal jūdi wal jabarūt, wa ahlal ʿafwi war raḥmah, wa ahlat taqwā wal maghfirah, asʾaluka biḥaqqi hādhal yawm, alladhī jaʿaltahu lilmuslimīna ʿīdā, wa limuḥammadin ṣallallāhu ʿalayhi wa ālihi wa sallam, dhukhraw wa sharafan wa karāmatan wa mazīdā, an tuṣalliya ʿalā muḥammadin wa āli muḥammad, wa an tudkhilanī fī kulli khayrin adkhalta fīhi muḥammadan wa āla muḥammad, wa an tukhrijanī min kulli sūʾin akhrajta minhu muḥammadan wa āla muḥammad, ṣalawātuka ʿalayhi wa ʿalayhim, allāhumma innī asʾaluka khayra mā saʾalaka bihi ʿibādukaṣ ṣāliḥūn, wa aʿūdhu bika mimmas taʿādha minhu ʿibādukal mukhlaṣūn."

Translation; "O God! Worthy of supremacy and greatness, and worthy of magnanimity and omnipotence, and worthy of pardoning and showing mercy, and worthy of being wary of and forgiving: I beseech You by the right of this day – which You have appointed to be an ʿĪd for the Muslims, and to be for Muḥammad, may God shower His blessings upon, and extend His salutations to, him and his progeny, [a source for] accumulating [Your blessings], and [a source of] honor, nobility, and increase [in Your blessings] – that You bless Muḥammad and the progeny of Muḥammad, and that You place me in every goodness in which You placed Muḥammad and the progeny of Muḥammad, and that You remove me from every evil from which You removed Muḥammad and the progeny of Muḥammad, may Your blessings be upon him and them. O God! I beseech You for the good for which Your righteous servants have beseeched You, and I seek protection in You from all that Your purified servants have sought Your protection."

Issue 688: There is no problem with shortening or prolonging the recitation of the supplications during the Qunūt of 'Īd prayers, but decreasing or increasing their number is not permissible.

Issue 689: If the worshiper has doubt about the number of takbīrs or Qunūts of the 'Īd prayer he is performing, and if he has not passed their designated place within the prayer, he should act on the doubt and assumption of the lesser number [of takbīrs or Qunūts] and act accordingly. If it becomes clear later that he had performed them correctly, then there is no problem.

Issue 690: If one forgets the recitation [of Sūrat al-Fātiḥah and the other Sūrah], takbīrs, or Qunūts during the 'Īd prayers, the prayer remains valid. However, if one forgets the bowing, prostrations, or Takbīrat al-Iḥrām [opening takbīr], then the prayer becomes invalid.

Issue 691: The 'Īd prayers for 'Īd al-Fiṭr and 'Īd al-Aḍḥa are not made up.

Congregational Prayer

Social cohesion in Islām is prominent in many religious obligations, including prayer. Establishing this act of worship in congregation paints a canvas of greatness, majesty, and grandeur, fostering a spirit of affection, unity, and cooperation among the believers. That is not to mention the abundant reward and immense blessings promised by God for those who establish congregational prayer. As much as there is an emphasis on and encouragement for congregational prayer, there is an equal amount of condemnation for neglecting it and abstaining from participation, to the extent that it is considered a sign of hypocrisy. Congregational prayer also serves as a training ground for obedience to the Master, venerating the purified and righteous, and adhering to orderliness in action when emulating them.

The Recommendation of Congregational Prayer

Issue 692: Congregational prayer is recommended in the daily prayers, with emphasis reported particularly on its recommendation for the Fajr prayer and the two evening prayers.

Issue 693: Participation in congregational prayer is recommended for everyone, but it is emphasized for those close to the mosque and those who can hear its call to prayer.

Issue 694: It is recommended that those who have prayed individually repeat their prayer in the congregation if the congregational prayer is established afterward. If it becomes evident later that his prayer was invalid, the second prayer suffices [the congregational prayer] in its place.

Issue 695: If someone is engaged in performing an individual obligatory prayer consisting of three or four units and the congregational prayer begins, and he is not sure whether he will catch up with it after completing his prayer, it is recommended for him to switch his prayer intention to a recommended prayer [nāfilah] and complete it with two units if he has not yet entered the third unit of his obligatory prayer, and then join the congregation.

Issue 696: If parents instruct their child to perform congregational prayer, neglecting it would cause harm to the parents. Based on obligatory precaution, the child must take part in congregational prayer.

Issue 697: Those afflicted with obsessive compulsiveness in prayer are not obligated to perform congregational prayer unless their condition reaches a level that disrupts the prayer or if their repetition of the remembrances prevents them from following the imām [leader of the prayer], thus nullifying the prayer.

Instance Where Congregational Prayer is Permissible

Issue 698: Congregational prayer is permissible for all obligatory daily prayers. If the imām is performing one of the daily prayers, it is permissible for followers to emulate him in the same or any other daily prayer.

Issue 699: If the imām repeats his prayer as a precaution, it is not permissible for the follower to emulate him unless the follower also repeats his prayer as a precaution and the precautionary aspect of his prayer corresponds to that of the imām.

Issue 700: If the imām is performing one of the obligatory daily prayers, it is permissible for the follower to emulate him in making up any of the obligatory daily prayers.

Issue 701: If the imām is engaged in making up one of the obligatory daily prayers, it is permissible for the follower to emulate him either in performing the obligatory daily prayers or making them up. However, if the make-up prayer is precautionary, meaning that it is performed to make up for a missed prayer that was not certainly missed, whether for oneself or another, it is not permissible to emulate him.

Issue 702: If someone is repeating the daily prayer as a precaution (whether the precaution is recommended or obligatory), it is permissible for him to emulate someone performing an obligatory prayer (either as the fulfillment of duty [ada] or as make-up [qaḍā']).

Issue 703: If the imām's or the follower's prayer is shortened [qaṣr], the congregation is valid, and they both receive the reward of congregational prayer.

Issue 704: Congregational prayer is obligatory for the Friday prayer, and individual prayer is invalid here.

Issue 705: It is permissible for the imām to lead congregational prayer for the obligatory daily prayers again only once, provided the followers in the second congregation differ from those of the first congregation.

Instances Where Congregational Prayer is Not Permissible

Issue 706: Congregational prayer is not valid for the circumambulation around the Ka'bah.

Issue 707: Congregational prayer is not permitted for any of the recommended prayers except for the 'Īd al-Fiṭr and 'Īd al-Aḍḥa prayers (recommended during the period of occultation) and the prayer for seeking rain [istisqā'] to ask for rainfall.

Issue 708: Congregational prayer is not permitted for the 'Īd al-Ghadīr prayer.

Issue 709: If one does not know whether the prayer led by the imām is obligatory or recommended, it is not permissible to emulate him.

Issue 710: It is not permissible to emulate an imām who performs precautionary units of prayer (extra units of prayer that the worshiper is obliged to perform in case of doubt about the number of units) in the daily prayers. Additionally, it is not permissible to emulate someone performing the daily obligatory prayers when performing precautionary units.

Conditions for the Imām of the Congregation

Issue 711: It is a condition for the imām of the congregation to be sane, just, and a Twelver Shīʿa, be born legitimately, be an adult based on obligatory precaution, perform his prayers correctly, and be male if the follower is male.

Issue 712: If all the followers are women, it is permissible for their imām to be a woman.

Issue 713: It is not permissible for someone praying while standing to emulate someone praying while sitting or lying down.

Issue 714: It is permissible for someone praying while sitting to emulate someone who is also praying while sitting.

Issue 715: Emulating someone who performs tayammum (dry ablution) or ablution with a cast or impure clothing or body is permissible due to an excuse.

Issue 716: If there is doubt whether the imām of the congregation—who is believed to be just—is still just or not, it is permissible to emulate him.

Conditions of the Congregational Prayer

Issue 717: In congregational prayer, it is obligatory to observe the following conditions:

1. The follower should not be ahead of the imām in position, and it is preferable for him to lag slightly behind.

2. The imām's position should not be higher than the followers, although a minor difference (less than a cubit) does not invalidate the prayer.

3. There should not be a large distance between the imām and the followers or between the rows of worshipers.

4. There should be no barrier between the follower and the imām or between the rows of worshipers, such as a wall or curtain. However, having a curtain between the rows of men and women is permissible.

Issue 718: If congregational prayer is established on sloping ground, and the imām's position is on the elevated part, as long as the incline is minimal to the extent that it can be considered level ground, then there is no problem.

Issue 719: If the follower's position is elevated, and the elevation is within the customary range, such as the courtyard or the mosque's roof, and not from multiple-story buildings, then the congregation is valid.

Issue 720: It is an obligatory precaution that the distance between the place of prostration of the follower and the position of the imām, as well as between the front row's position and the place of prostration of the rear row, does not exceed one long step (approximately one meter).

Issue 721: If the follower is not connected to the imām from the front in the congregational prayer, but he is connected to him through another follower, either to his right or left only, the prayer remains valid.

Issue 722: If the distance between the follower and the imām, or between the follower and another follower through whom he is connected to the imām, exceeds one long step, the connection to the congregation is severed, and his prayer becomes individual.

Issue 723: If the connection in the congregation is through a child who has not yet reached puberty, if it is known that his prayer is valid, then emulating him and praying in the congregation is permissible.

Issue 724: If all individuals in the front row have completed their prayer or have all separated, if the distance to the next row is not more than one large step, the connection to the congregation remains valid, and the congregation is considered valid. If the distance exceeds this amount, their prayers become individual unless those whose prayers have ended return to follow again without a gap.

Issue 725: If the imām's prayer is invalidated or ends before the followers' prayer, such as if he is a traveler, then it is permissible for the followers to appoint one of them (who fulfills the conditions for leading the congregation) to lead them, and they complete their prayer following him.

Duty of the Follower in Congregational Prayer

Issue 726: It is not permissible for the follower to perform the initial Takbīrat al-Iḥrām before the imām. Rather, it is an obligatory precaution not to perform the takbīr before the imām completes his takbīr.

Issue 727: After the imām's takbīr, if those praying in the front row are prepared for prayer and about to say the takbīr, then it is permissible for the one standing in the back row to say the takbīr.

Issue 728: It is an obligatory precaution for the follower not to recite Sūrat al-Fātiḥah and the other Sūrah in the first two units of Ẓuhr and ʿAṣr prayers, and it is recommended for him to engage in remembrance of God instead of them.

Issue 729: In Fajr prayer and the first units of Maghrib and ʿIshāʾ prayers, if the follower hears the imām reciting Sūrat al-Fātiḥah and the other Sūrah, even if only as a murmur, it is not permissible for him to recite Sūrat al-Fātiḥah and the other Sūrah. Moreover, it is an obligatory precaution not to recite Sūrat al-Fātiḥah and the other Sūrah upon hearing only some of their words. However, if he does not hear the imām's voice, it is recommended for him to recite Sūrat al-Fātiḥah and the other Sūrah in a whisper, and if he accidentally recites them aloud, his prayer remains valid.

Issue 730: Besides Sūrat al-Fātiḥah and the other Sūrah, the follower must perform all the remembrances and utterances of prayer by himself. However, if he joins the congregation in the third or fourth unit of the imām's prayer, then he must recite Sūrat al-Fātiḥah and the other Sūrah.

Issue 731: If one makes a mistake in identifying the imām of the congregation and prays behind someone thinking he is, for example, "ʿAlī," but it becomes clear after the prayer that he is actually "Aḥmad," and if "Aḥmad" is just. His following was not limited to a specific imām of the congregation, then the congregation remains valid.

However, suppose his following was limited to a specific person (ʿAlī). In that case, his congregation is invalid, and if he did not add a pillar [rukn] act to his prayer, it can be considered valid as his prayer.

Issue 732: There is no problem with the follower preceding or lagging behind the imām in the utterances of prayer,[45] except for Takbīrat al-Iḥrām, the ruling of which was mentioned previously. It is recommended precaution not to precede the imām in utterances other than Takbīrat al-Iḥrām if he hears what the imām says or knows when he says it.

Issue 733: The follower must perform the actions of prayer relatively at the same time as the imām or slightly afterward, intentionally preceding the imām or lagging behind him considerably—in such a way that it can no longer be said that he is following the imām— is not permissible.

Issue 734: If the follower inadvertently bows before the imām of the congregation, he must raise his head from the bowing position, then bow again with the imām, and complete the prayer with him; his congregational prayer is

---

[45] Prayer is divided into two parts:

1. Utterances of prayer: These are the parts that are recited in prayer, such as Takbīrat al-Iḥrām, Sūrat al-Fātiḥah, the other Sūrah, remembrance of God, tashahhud, and taslīm.
2. Acts of prayer: These are the actions performed in prayer, such as standing, bowing, prostrating, and sitting after the prostration.

thus valid. If he does return from the bowing position, his prayer is valid instead.

Issue 735: If he advertently raises his head from the bowing position before the imām, and if the imām is still bowing, he must return to the bowing. In this case, adding to this pillar [bowing] does not invalidate the prayer. However, his prayer is invalid if the follower bends again to bow, but the imām rises before he can reach the full bowing position again.

Issue 736: If he inadvertently prostrates before the imām, he must raise his head from prostration, then prostrate with the imām, and his congregational prayer thus remains valid.

Issue 737: If he inadvertently raises his head from prostration before the imām and finds the imām still in prostration, he returns to prostration but does not catch up with the imām's prostration; his prayer remains valid. However, if this happens in both prostrations, his prayer is invalidated.

Issue 738: If he inadvertently raises his head from bowing or prostration before the imām and does not return to bowing or prostration either inadvertently or due to assuming he cannot catch up with the imām, his prayer remains valid.

Issue 739: If the imām inadvertently performs Qunūt in a unit where it is not performed, the follower must not perform Qunūt. However, he cannot bow before the imām; rather, he waits until the imām finishes his Qunūt and continues his prayer.

Issue 740: If the imām accidentally recites tashahhud in a unit without reciting, the follower must not recite tashahhud. However, he cannot rise before the imām; rather, he waits until the imām completes his tashahhud and continues the prayer with him.

Duties of the Follower When Joining in Different Rakʿahs [Units of Prayer]

Joining in the first unit:

Issue 741: If the follower joins the imām in the first or second unit of prayer, then the obligation of reciting Sūrat al-Fātiḥah and the other Sūrah is lifted from him in that unit.

Issue 742: If the imām is standing, and the follower does not know which unit of prayer he is in, he can emulate him, but he must recite Sūrat al-Fātiḥah and the other Sūrah with the intention of seeking nearness to God and his congregational prayer remains valid even if it becomes clear later that the imām was in the first or second unit.

Issue 743: If the follower did not recite Sūrat al-Fātiḥah and the other Sūrah assuming that the imām was in the first or second unit, but then it becomes apparent after the bowing that he was in the third or fourth unit, then his prayer remains valid. However, he realizes that before bowing, then he must recite Sūrat al-Fātiḥah and the other Sūrah; if there is not enough time, he should suffice with Sūrat al-Fātiḥah and catch up with the imām in bowing.

Issue 744: If one joins the congregation at the beginning of the prayer or during the recitation of Sūrat al-Fātiḥah or the other Sūrah, and the imām raises his head before bowing, then his congregational prayer is valid, and he must bow and catch up with the imām.

Joining in bowing:

Issue 745: If one joins the congregation during the imām's bowing, then one of the following situations may occur:

1. If the follower reaches the point of bowing while the imām is still bowing, his congregational prayer is valid. It counts as a complete unit of prayer for him, even if the imām has already recited the remembrance.

2. Suppose the follower reaches the full bowing position while the imām is rising from bowing or already standing. In that case, his prayer is valid,

and the first unit of prayer is counted for him. He must complete his prayer.

3. If the follower reaches the full bowing position and doubts whether he caught up with the imām's bowing, his prayer is valid, and the first unit of prayer is counted for him. He must complete his prayer.

4. If the imām raises his head before the follower reaches the full bowing position, the follower must continue praying individually.

Joining in the second unit:

Issue 746: If the follower joins in the second unit of prayer, considering the prayer of the imām, there are three scenarios:

1. If the imām's prayer is a two-unit prayer, it is recommended that the follower recite the Qunūt with the imām. He can either rise during the imām's tashahhud and complete the rest of the prayer individually or withdraw until the imām recites the salutation [taslīm] and then rise.

2. Suppose the imām's prayer is a three-unit prayer. In that case, it is recommended to recite the Qunūt and tashahhud with the imām, and it is an obligatory precaution to withdraw during the

imām's tashahhud, then rise with him, and recite Sūrat al-Fātiḥah and the other Sūrah. If the imām does not allow enough time for reciting the other Sūrah, the follower should suffice with Sūrat al-Fātiḥah and catch up with the imām in bowing. After the two prostrations, he should recite tashahhud for his second unit. If his prayer is also three units, he can rise when the imām is reciting taslīm and complete his prayer, or he can withdraw until the imām finishes reciting taslīm, then rise to complete the third unit.

3. If the imām's prayer is four-unit, the follower performs the first unit as mentioned in the previous scenario. In his second unit (third unit of the imām), after the two prostrations, he recites the obligatory portion of tashahhud, then rises and performs the third unit. If the imām does not allow him time to recite the four tasbīhs three times, he should suffice with once, catch up with the imām in bowing, and complete his prayer in the manner previously mentioned.

Joining in the third or fourth unit:

Issue 747: If one joins the imām in the third or fourth unit of prayer, he must recite Sūrat al-Fātiḥah and the other Sūrah. If the imām does not give him enough time for the other Sūrah, he should suffice with Sūrat al-Fātiḥah alone and catch up with the imām in bowing.

Issue 748: If the follower knows that if he recites the other Sūrah, he will not be able to catch up with the imām in bowing, he must leave it. If he recites it and fails to catch up with the imām in bowing, his prayer turns into individual prayer.

Issue 749: If the imām is in the third or fourth unit of prayer, and the follower knows that if he joins and recites Sūrat al-Fātiḥah, he will not catch up with the imām in bowing, then it is an obligatory precaution for him to wait until the imām bows, then join him.

Issue 750: If one reaches the congregation while the imām is busy reciting the final tashahhud of the prayer, and if he desires to attain the reward of the congregation, he should make the intention, and after Takbīrat al-Iḥrām, he should sit, recite the tashahhud of the prayer with the imām, but he should not recite the taslīm. He should wait until the imām completes the taslīm of his prayer, then rise after that, completing the prayer, meaning he recites Sūrat al-Fātiḥah and the other Sūrah, considering it as his first unit. This action is specific to the final tashahhud of the congregational prayer to attain its reward, and it cannot be done in the tashahhud of the second unit of the three-unit or four-unit prayers.

Switching From Congregational to Individual Prayer

Issue 751: It is permissible for a person to switch his intention to an individual prayer intention during congregational prayer, and he completes his prayer individually, even if he intended to do that from the beginning of the prayer. However, it is recommended precaution not to intend that from the beginning of the prayer.

Issue 752: If the follower intends to pray individually after the imām completes the recitation [of Sūrat al-Fātiḥah and the other Sūrah], then he does not need to recite. However, if he intends to pray individually during the recitation and then changes his intention after the completion of Sūrat al-Fātiḥah, he is not obligated to recite it. But suppose he changes his intention during Sūrat al-Fātiḥah or the other Sūrah. In that case, it is an obligatory precaution for him to restart his recitation from the beginning with the intention of absolute nearness to God (not with the intention of repetition).

Issue 753: If one intends to pray individually during congregational prayer, it is an obligatory precaution not to return to the intention of the congregation again, even if only a short time has passed. Likewise, if one hesitates between the intention of praying individually and not, it is an obligatory precaution to complete the prayer individually.

The Recommendations [Mustaḥabb] and Detestables [Makrūh] Aspects of Congregational Prayer

Issue 754: It is preferable for the imām to stand in the middle of the row and for people of knowledge, perfection, and piety to stand in the front row.

Issue 755: It is recommended in congregational prayer to align the rows, not to create gaps between individuals in the same row, and to ensure alignment between the shoulders.

Issue 756: It is recommended for the followers to stand up after the phrase "Qad Qāmat aṣ-Ṣalāt" (the prayer has been established).

Issue 757: It is recommended that the imām of the congregation consider the condition of the weakest followers and not rush until they catch up.

Issue 758: It is recommended for the imām of the congregation, during the prayers that necessitate aloud recitation, to raise his voice in reciting Sūrat al-Fātiḥah, the other Sūrahs, and the remembrances that are recited aloud, such that others can hear him, but he must not raise his voice beyond the commonly accepted limit.

Issue 759: If the imām, while in bowing, becomes aware of someone intending to join the congregation, it is recommended that he prolong the bowing double than usual, then rise, even if he becomes aware of another person intending to join.

Issue 760: It is detestable [makruh] for a follower to stand alone while space is available in the congregation's rows.

Issue 761: It is detestable for a follower to raise his voice when uttering the remembrances to a level where the imām can hear.

Friday Prayer

The Friday prayer is a weekly assembly for Muslims focusing on the "remembrance of God" and "worshiping the Creator." The sermons of the Friday prayer imām include admonition and purification of the self, enlightenment, and education. This prayer falls within the affairs of the Islāmic government, carrying political and governmental significance as well. It is also a manifestation of the greatness of the Islāmic nation and the strength of religious governance.

The fact that there is a Sūrah in the Qur'ān named "al-Jumu'ah" [Friday], wherein God commands Muslims to strive to perform this prayer, is evidence of its importance. The Friday prayer unites Muslims, disrupts the enemy's media influence and mechanism, and also serves as a means to understand the social functions and issues of the Islāmic world. Furthermore, it serves as a form of mobilization of forces, and continuous attendance at these ceremonies signifies solidarity with the Islāmic nation and the goals of the Islāmic system.

Issue 762: Friday prayer—which is held on Fridays in place of the Ẓuhr prayer—in the present time (the era of the Imām's occultation عجل الله تعالى فرجه الشريف), is a *Wajib Takhyīrī*, meaning the accountable person has the option, in the fulfillment of the obligatory prayer of Friday noon, to choose between performing Ẓuhr prayer and Friday prayer. It is an obligatory precaution in this era—during which the Islāmic government of justice was established in Iran—not to abandon the Friday prayer as much as possible.

Issue 763: Not participating in the Friday prayer due to not caring about it is religiously disapproved.

Conditions of the Friday Prayer

Issue 764: Conditions for the validity of the Friday prayer:

1. Congregation.
2. The number of worshippers should not be less than five individuals (the imām and four followers).
3. Observing all the essential conditions of congregational prayer, such as connecting the rows.

4. The distance between [the location of] one Friday prayer and the adjacent one should not be less than one Farsakh.[46]

Issue 765: It is permissible for a traveler who performs qaṣr prayers to participate in the Friday prayer and to perform the Friday prayer instead of the Ẓuhr prayer.

Issue 766: The criterion for the distance separating two Friday prayers is the place of prayer establishment, not the town in which it is held.

Issue 767: If two Friday prayers are held with a distance of less than one Farsakh between them, the one held first is valid, and the second is invalid. If both were held at the same time, both are invalidated.

Conditions for the Imām of the Friday Prayer

Issue 768: The imām of the Friday prayer must meet all the valid conditions for leading the congregation, such as being just.

Issue 769: If someone was initially confident in the justice of the Friday prayer imām when following him but later doubts or becomes certain of his injustice after the prayer, the previous prayers he performed emulating that imām remain valid.

---

[46] One Farsakh is approximately 5125 meters.

Issue 770: If the appointment of an individual as the imām of the Friday prayer instills trust and confidence in his justice, then this is sufficient for the validity of following him in prayer.

Timing of the Friday Prayer

Issue 771: The timing of the Friday prayer starts from the beginning of the sun's descent from its zenith [Zawāl] (the beginning of Ẓuhr), and it is an obligatory precaution not to delay it past the prime time of Ẓuhr prayer conventionally.

Issue 772: It is permissible for the imām of the Friday prayer to deliver both sermons before the call to Ẓuhr prayer.

Method of Performing the Friday Prayer

Issue 773: Friday prayer consists of two units of prayer, preceded by two sermons delivered by the Friday imām before the prayer.

Issue 774: It is an obligatory precaution to recite the Qur'ān aloud during the Friday prayer. It is recommended in the first unit to recite Sūrat al-Jumuʿah and in the second unit Sūrat al-Munāfiqūn. Two Qunūt supplications are also recommended, one in the first unit before bowing and the second in the second after bowing.

Obligations Upon the Imām of Friday Prayer

Issue 775: It is obligatory for the imām of Friday prayer (and no one else) to deliver the sermons while standing. If he cannot deliver them while standing, it becomes obligatory for another person to deliver the sermons and lead the Friday prayer.

Issue 776: It is obligatory for the imām of Friday prayer to sit briefly between the first and second sermons.

Issue 777: It is not permissible for the Friday sermon speaker to deliver the sermons in a low voice. Rather, he should raise his voice so that at least the minimum required number of people for the Friday prayer (four individuals) can hear him. Moreover, it is recommended that precautions be taken during preaching and advising people to have piety, to make his voice reach all present, even if it requires a microphone.

Issue 778: It is obligatory for the Friday sermon speaker in the first sermon to praise and extol God, send blessings upon the Prophet ﷺ, advise people to be pious, and recite a short chapter from the Qur'ān. Similarly, in the second sermon, he should praise and extol God and send blessings upon the Prophet ﷺ. It is also an obligatory precaution to advise people to be pious and recite a short chapter from the Qur'ān. After sending blessings upon the Prophet ﷺ in the second sermon, it is recommended precaution to send blessings upon the infallible Imāms عليهم السلام and seek forgiveness for the believers.

Obligations Upon the Worshipers in the Friday Prayer

Issue 779: It is an obligatory precaution for the worshipers to listen attentively to the imām's two sermons and refrain from speaking.

Issue 780: It is recommended that the worshipers face the imām during the sermon and not turn their faces away from the Qiblah more than what is permissible during prayer.

Issue 781: If a worshiper misses both sermons of the Friday prayer, for example, joining only during the prayer and following the Friday prayer imām, his prayer is valid, and it substitutes for the Ẓuhr prayer. Even if he joins the Friday prayer before the bowing of the last unit, he can emulate the intention of the Friday prayer, and he should perform the second unit in the same manner as the second unit of the Friday prayer. This prayer suffices in place of the Ẓuhr prayer for him.

Miscellaneous Issues Regarding the Friday Prayer

Issue 782: Friday prayer is an Islāmic ritual that manifests Muslim unity. Engaging in any action that leads to discord among believers and disrupts their unity is not permissible.

Issue 783: There is no problem emulating a person other than the imām of the Friday prayer in the ʿAṣr prayer on Friday.

Issue 784: Whoever misses the Friday prayer may perform the Ẓuhr prayer in its prime time, and it is not obligatory to wait until the Friday prayer concludes.

Issue 785: There is no problem establishing the Ẓuhr prayer in the congregation while the Friday prayer is being held elsewhere nearby. However, since this action may lead to the dispersion of the believers' rows, negligence regarding the Friday prayer, or disrespecting the imām of Friday, it is prudent not to establish such a congregation. Instead, it is necessary to avoid it if it entails corruption or what is impermissible.

aṣ-Ṣawm | Fasting

Fasting is one of the most important practices for self-discipline in the heavenly religions, and God has also decreed it for the previous nations. Among the blessings of fasting are attaining a spiritual state, purifying the soul, feeling hunger and thirst, awakening empathy for the impoverished, strengthening willpower, and resilience against the desires of the self. It also serves as a reminder of the hunger and thirst on the Day of Judgment. Furthermore, there is no doubt about the important role of fasting in maintaining bodily health and regulating the body's reception and consumption of food. Prophetic traditions point to this effect, where we read: "Fast so that you become healthy." This is in addition to the great reward God ﷻ promised the fasting individuals.

On the other hand, among the blessings of this act of worship is the impact of fasting in curbing sexual desires, disciplining the soul, training it to endure difficult conditions and scarcity of food, and nurturing individuals with refined will and disciplined souls; one equipped with patience, resilience, and conviction. In addition to the obligatory fasting in the month of Ramaḍān, the devoted friends of God used to fast many of the recommended days, believing that they bring them closer to God ﷻ.

Issue 786: Fasting in the sacred Islāmic law is for a person to abstain from the things that break the fast—which will be detailed later—from the true dawn[47] until sunset with the intention of obeying the command of God ﷻ.

Conditions for the Obligation and Validity of Fasting

Issue 787: The conditions for the obligation of fasting are as follows:

1. Having reached puberty.
2. Being sane of mind.
3. Being able to.
4. Not being unconscious.
5. Not being a traveler.

---

[47] True dawn versus false dawn: False dawn is light that appears in the sky before true dawn. Instead of spreading horizontally across the horizon, it shines vertically upwards. True dawn is when soft white sunlight touching the horizon's surface appears and spreads across the horizon. Therefore, observing true dawn requires viewing from an open, dark, east-facing horizon. And that is why seeing it from inside cities is very difficult. Hence, since identifying true dawn accurately is difficult, and in order to observe precaution concerning fasting, one must abstain from food and drink at the beginning of the morning call to prayer [ādhān], and prayer is delayed ten minutes after the beginning of the ādhān. This time is applied in a country like Iran, and the more north you go in countries, the more this time increases.

6. Not being a woman in menstruation or postpartum bleeding.

7. Fasting is not harmful [to the person].

8. Fasting is not the cause of undue hardship.

Issue 788: Fasting is obligatory for anyone who meets the aforementioned conditions. Thus, fasting is not obligatory on non-pubescent children, the insane, the unconscious, those unable to fast, the traveler, menstruating or postpartum women, and those for whom fasting would cause harm or undue hardship (severe hardship).

Issue 789: If a child reaches puberty before the dawn prayer during Ramaḍān, it becomes obligatory for them to fast. However, if they reach puberty after the dawn prayer, fasting that day is not obligatory for them.

Issue 790: Girls who have newly reached puberty[48] must fast, and it is not permissible to refrain from fasting due to mere difficulty or physical weakness unless it would cause them harm or severe hardship.

Issue 791: The fasting of menstruating or postpartum women is not valid, even if they menstruate or give birth

---

[48] According to popular opinion, girls reach puberty when they complete nine lunar years (i.e., eight years, eight months, and twenty-three days according to the solar or Gregorian calendar).

moments before sunset or if they become pure moments after dawn.

Issue 792: If someone knows that fasting would harm them, or if there is a reasonable possibility of harm, he is not obligated to fast, and in some cases, it may be forbidden, whether certainty in this regard is achieved or there is fear of the harm of fasting from personal experience, a trustworthy doctor's words, or another rational source. Even if he fasted, his fast was not valid unless it was done with the intention of seeking closeness to God, and it later became clear that it would not cause harm.

Issue 793: If someone believes fasting does not harm him but later finds out after sunset that it does, his fast is invalid, and he must make up for it.

Issue 794: Determining the effect of fasting in causing or exacerbating illness, incapacity to fast, or fasting being harmful is the responsibility of the Islāmically accountable person [mukallaf]. If a doctor says fasting is harmful but does not provide certainty or reasonable fear of harm, or if the mukallaf knows through experience that it is not harmful, fasting is obligatory. Similarly, if a doctor says fasting is not harmful, but the person knows it would harm him or has a reasonable fear of harm, he must refrain from fasting, which is forbidden for him.

Issue 795: If a sick person recovers during the day in Ramaḍān, he is not obligated to make the intention of fasting and fasting that day. However, if this happens before noon and he has not consumed anything that breaks the fast, it is recommended precaution for him to make the intention of fasting, and he must make up for it after Ramaḍān.

Issue 796: For recommended fasting to be valid, one must not have any missed obligatory fasting days from Ramaḍān to make up for, and it is an obligatory precaution that he is not responsible for fasting another obligatory fast.

Issue 797: If someone has obligatory fasting to make up for and is unaware of the validity of recommended fasting due to his responsibility of the make-up fasting if he fasts with the intention of recommendation, his fast is invalid, and it does not count towards making up for the obligatory fasting either.

Issue 798: If someone is unsure whether he has obligatory fasting to make up for or not, and he fasts with the intention of what is obligated upon him (which is broader than making up for missed fasting or recommended fasting), and he has obligatory fasting to make up for, then his fasting counts towards making up for the obligatory fasting.

Issue 799: If someone has obligatory fasting to make up for and forgets and fasts with the intention of recommendation, if he remembers during the day, his recommended fast becomes invalid. However, if he remembers before noon, he can make the intention to make up for the missed fasting of Ramaḍān, but if it is after noon, intending to make up for it is not valid as well.

Obligations of Fasting

Issue 800: When it comes to fasting, one must observe two matters:

1. Intention.

2. Avoiding what breaks one's fast.

Intention

Issue 801: Fasting must be accompanied by intention, just like all other acts of worship, meaning that abstaining from eating, drinking, and other invalidators of fasting must be made with the intention of obeying the command of God ﷻ. Mere intention and determination for that suffice, and verbalizing it is unnecessary.

Issue 802: It is not obligatory to specify the type of fasting in the fasting month of Ramaḍān; rather, mere intention to fast is sufficient. However, outside of Ramaḍān, it is necessary to specify the type of fasting, even if in a general manner. For example, suppose someone has no fasting to fulfill except for the obligatory make-up fasting. In that case, he must specify the intention for the make-up fasting or intend fasting what is due upon him in general (i.e., whatever is obligatory upon him). If someone has multiple types of fasting to fulfill, such as make-up fasting and fasting obligated by vows, he must specify which one he intends to fast.

Issue 803: If the accountable person knows that he has fasting to observe but does not know its type, he can make the intention of [fasting] whatever is incumbent upon him.

Issue 804: It is not obligatory to fast on a day of doubt,[49] wherein it is uncertain whether it is the last day of Shaʿbān or the first day of Ramaḍān. If someone intends to fast on that day, he cannot intend to fast for Ramaḍān. Instead, he can intend fasting as a recommendation for the last day of Shaʿbān or intend make-up fasting. If it later becomes clear that it is indeed Ramaḍān, his fasting is counted for Ramaḍān, and there is no obligation to make it up. If it becomes clear during the day that it is Ramaḍān, he must

---

[49] If the crescent of the month is not sighted by the sunset of the twenty-ninth day of the lunar month due to clouds or other reasons, or if there is a disagreement regarding the sighting of the crescent, that day is termed the day of doubt. If the doubt occurs between the end of Shaʿbān and the beginning of Ramaḍān, the day is considered the last day of Shaʿbān, and fasting on that day is permissible with the intention of recommended fasting or make-up fasting. It is not permissible to intend fasting for Ramaḍān on that day. However, if doubt occurs between the end of Ramaḍān and the beginning of Shawwāl, the day is considered the last day of Ramaḍān, and fasting on that day is obligatory.

change his intention to fasting Ramaḍān from that moment onward.

The Intention of the Month of Ramaḍān

Issue 805: Since fasting in the month of Ramaḍān begins from the beginning of dawn, it is also necessary that one's intention is not delayed until after that moment. It is preferable to intend fasting before the break of dawn.

Issue 806: On every night of Ramaḍān, a person can intend to fast for the following day, but it is preferable on the first night of the month to intend to fast for the entire month and renew the intention every night.

Issue 807: If someone intends to fast the next day from the beginning of the night, then falls asleep and does not wake up before dawn, or becomes engaged in something and forgets about the arrival of dawn, then becomes aware of that afterward, his fast is valid.

Issue 808: In the month of Ramaḍān, intending fasting for other than Ramaḍān is not valid, except for a traveler who cannot fast Ramaḍān and has made a vow to fast a recommended fasting during travel. In this case, it is valid to intend fasting for his vow in Ramaḍān.[50]

---

[50] Of course, fasting for a vow in the month of Ramaḍān does not count as part of Ramaḍān fasting, and the person must make up for that day later.

Issue 809: If someone intentionally decides on a night in Ramaḍān not to fast until the break of dawn, his fast is not valid even if he intends to during the day. However, he must refrain from what breaks the fast until sunset and make up for that day after Ramaḍān.

Issue 810: If someone forgets to fast in Ramaḍān due to forgetfulness or ignorance and remembers during the day if he has already committed what breaks the fast, then he cannot make the intention of fasting, whether he remembered before or after noon. If he has not committed any acts that break the fast, and he remembers after noon, his intention for fasting is not valid, and in both cases, he must refrain from what breaks the fast until sunset. If he remembers before noon, it is an obligatory precaution to make the intention of fasting, and he must make up for that day later as well.

Intention of Fasting Outside the Month of Ramaḍān

Issue 811: If a person has obligatory fasting for a specific day other than Ramaḍān, such as a vow to fast on a particular day, and intentionally fails to make the intention of fasting until dawn, his fast is invalidated. However, if he forgot the intention and remembered it before noon, he could still have made the intention of fasting.

Issue 812: In non-specific fasting, such as expiatory fasting or make-up fasting, if one fails to make the intention before noon (intentionally or inadvertently), and he has not consumed anything that breaks the fast, he can still make the intention, and his fast is valid. However, intending to fast in the afternoon or later is not valid.

Issue 813: Intending recommended fasting is valid at any time during the day, provided that one has not consumed anything that breaks the fast until that moment.

Continuity in Intention

Issue 814: In specific obligatory fasting, such as fasting in Ramaḍān or a vowed fast for a specific day, continuity in intention from the break of dawn until sunset is required. Therefore, if someone retracts his intention during the day and intends to discontinue fasting, his fast is invalidated even if he reverts to the intention to continue fasting again. Of course, refraining from consuming anything that breaks the fast until sunset is obligatory in Ramaḍān.

Issue 815: In specific obligatory fasting, if there is hesitation about whether to continue fasting or not or if one intends to commit something that invalidates the fast but does not do it, it is safer to complete the fast and make up for it later.

Issue 816: In recommended and non-specific obligatory fasting (which is not specifically tied to a particular day), if someone intends to break the fast or intends to commit something that invalidates the fast, or if there is hesitation and he has not committed anything that invalidates the fast, he can renew his intention to fast before noon in non-specific obligatory fasting and before sunset in recommended fasting.

Avoiding what breaks one's fast:

Issue 817: There are nine invalidators of fasting:

1. Eating and drinking.

2. Sexual intercourse.

3. Masturbation.

4. Remaining in a state of major ritual impurity [janābah], menstruation, or postpartum bleeding until the time of dawn prayer.

5. Applying liquid enema

6. Vomiting.

7. Uttering falsehood against God, His Messenger, or the infallible Imāms ﷺ (based on obligatory precaution).

8. Inhaling thick dust directly into the throat (based on obligatory precaution).

9. Submerging the entire head underwater (based on obligatory precaution).

Eating and Drinking:

Issue 818: If a fasting person intentionally eats or drinks something, knowing that it would invalidate his fast, whether it is something commonly consumed as food or drink or something else, such as paper or cloth, and whether it is a large or small amount, like water droplets or crumbs of bread, his fast is invalidated.

Issue 819: If a fasting person inadvertently eats or drinks something, his fast is not invalidated, whether the fasting is obligatory or recommended.

Issue 820: If a fasting person intentionally swallows food particles stuck between his teeth, his fast is invalidated. However, if he was unaware of the presence of the food between his teeth or if he did not swallow it intentionally and consciously, then his fast remains valid.

Issue 821: Swallowing saliva does not invalidate the fast.

Issue 822: Swallowing phlegm that originates from the head or chest and does not reach the mouth cavity does not invalidate the fast. However, if it reaches the mouth cavity, it is an obligatory precaution to avoid swallowing it.

Issue 823: Based on obligatory precaution, the fasting person should avoid strengthening injections, injections administered through veins, and all types of intravenous fluids. However, there is no objection to receiving nonnutritive injections in the muscle, such as antibiotics, painkillers, or sedatives, and there is also no objection to using medications applied to wounds.

Issue 824: Based on obligatory precaution, the fasting person should avoid inhaling smoke from various smoking materials and drugs absorbed by the body through the nose or under the tongue.

Issue 825: There is no objection to taking tablets, pills, or similar medications if necessary for treating an illness. However, this breaks the fast, and making up for the missed fasting days is necessary.

Issue 826: If saliva mixes with medication tablets placed under the tongue during use, his fast remains valid if the person spits it.

Issue 827: If a person realizes while eating that dawn has arrived, he must remove the morsel of food from his mouth. If he swallows it, his fast is invalidated.

Issue 828: Bleeding from the mouth does not invalidate the fast, but precautions should be taken to prevent it from reaching the throat.

Issue 829: If gum bleeding and blood from the teeth becomes diluted in saliva (diminishes and disappears), it is considered pure, and swallowing does not invalidate the fast. Similarly, if one doubts the presence of blood in saliva, there is no objection to swallowing it, and his fast remains valid.

Issue 830: Chewing food for a child, tasting food, and the like which do not usually reach the throat do not invalidate the fast, even if it accidentally reaches the throat and is swallowed involuntarily. However, if the person knows from the outset that it will reach the throat, swallowing it would invalidate the fast.

Issue 831: It is not permissible for a person to break his fast due to weakness. However, if his weakness reaches an unusually unbearable level, he may break his fast and make up for it later.

Sexual Intercourse:

Issue 832: Sexual intercourse invalidates the fast even if ejaculation does not occur.

Issue 833: If someone forgets that he is fasting and engages in sexual intercourse, his fast is not invalidated. However, he must immediately cease the intercourse as soon as he remembers. Otherwise, his fast will be invalidated.

Masturbation.

Issue 834: If a fasting person intentionally engages in an act that leads to ejaculation, his fast is invalidated.

Issue 835: If someone performs an action with the intention of ejaculation but it does not occur, it is safer to complete the fast and make up for it later.

Issue 836: If ejaculation occurs involuntarily during sleep or awake, it does not invalidate the fast.

Issue 837: Iḥtilām (a nocturnal emission) during the day does not invalidate the fast, and even if a fasting person knows that he may experience this if he sleeps, he is allowed to sleep.

Issue 838: If a fasting person wakes up during ejaculation, he is not obligated to stop it.

Issue 839: If a fasting person experiences ejaculation while sleeping during the daytime in the month of Ramaḍān or any other fasting day, he is not obliged to rush to perform ritual purification [ghusl] immediately upon waking up.

Remaining in a state of major ritual impurity [janābah], menstruation, or postpartum bleeding until the time of dawn prayer:

Issue 840: If a person becomes ritually impure [in state of janābah] due to sexual activity during the night in Ramaḍān, he must perform ritual purification [ghusl; major ablution] before the Fajr prayer (break of dawn). His fast is invalidated if he intentionally delays performing ghusl until that time. However, he must refrain from consuming anything that breaks the fast until sunset.

Issue 841: If someone becomes ritually impure during the night in the month of Ramaḍān and remains in that state until Fajr without performing ghusl, whether intentionally or inadvertently (such as if he becomes ritually impure while asleep and remains asleep until Fajr), his fast remains valid.

Issue 842: If someone intends to observe a make-up fast and intentionally remains in a state of janābah until Fajr, his fast is invalidated. If he inadvertently delays performing ghusl until after Fajr, his fast is also invalidated based on obligatory precaution.

Issue 843: If someone becomes in a state of janābah during the night in Ramaḍān and knows that he will wake up before the Fajr call to prayer if he sleeps, if he intentionally decides not to perform ghusl or is indecisive about it, and then falls asleep without waking up, his fast is invalidated.

Issue 844: If someone becomes in a state of janābah while awake or wakes up after experiencing ejaculation during sleep and knows that he will not wake up in time to perform ghusl [ritual bath or major ablution] before Fajr, it is not permissible for him to sleep before performing ghusl. His fast is invalidated if he sleeps and does not perform a ghusl before the Fajr call to prayer. However, if he can wake up for the ghusl before Fajr and intends to do so but does not wake up, his fast remains valid. But if he falls asleep again after waking up and does not wake up until after Fajr, he must make up the fast of that day.

Issue 845: If someone forgets to perform major ablution [ghusl of janābah] after becoming in a state of janābah in Ramaḍān and wakes up in a state of janābah, his fast for that day is valid. However, if this forgetfulness continues for several days, he must make up for the fasting days he spent in this forgetfulness. However, the prayers [in the state of janābah] are invalid.

Issue 846: If someone is uncertain about whether remaining in a state of janābah invalidates the fast or not, and he observes fasting while in that state, then it is an obligatory precaution to consider his fast invalidated,[51] and he must make it up later. However, if he is certain that remaining in a state of janābah does not invalidate the fast, and he fasts based on this understanding, his fast is valid, although it would be good to observe precaution and make up for it.

Issue 847: If someone's duty requires him to perform ghusl at night in Ramaḍān if he is unable to do so due to time constraints or harm from the water and the like, he must perform tayammum (dry ablution) instead of ghusl before Fajr.

---

[51] In cases where the fast is invalidated based on obligatory precaution, the accountable person must continue his fast and make it up later.

Issue 848: If someone does not have time for ghusl or tayammum at night in Ramaḍān, and he becomes in a state of janābah, his fast is invalidated, and he must make up for it and provide expiation for deliberate breaking of the fast. However, if he has time only for tayammum, his fast is valid if he becomes in a state of janābah and performs tayammum before Fajr.

Issue 849: If someone must perform tayammum, it is permissible for him to become in a state of janābah at night in Ramaḍān, provided he has sufficient time for tayammum after becoming in a state of janābah.

Issue 850: If a woman menstruates or experiences postpartum bleeding and becomes pure before Fajr, she must perform a ghusl before Fajr. If she deliberately delays the ghusl, her fast is invalidated.

Issue 851: If a fasting woman experiences menstruation or gives birth, her fast is invalidated.

Issue 852: Fasting on that day is invalid if a woman becomes pure from menstruation or postpartum bleeding after the Fajr call to prayer.

Issue 853: If a woman forgets to perform ghusl after menstruation or postpartum bleeding but remembers later, her fasting during that period is valid, whether it is in Ramaḍān or not.

Applying liquid enema:

Issue 854: Injecting fluid enema invalidates the fast, even if it is for necessity or medical treatment. However, injecting solids poses no issue and does not invalidate the fast.

Vomiting:

Issue 855: If a fasting person intentionally induces vomiting, his fast is invalidated, even if he was compelled to do so due to illness or other reasons. However, if vomiting occurs inadvertently or involuntarily, his fast remains valid.

Issue 856: If something spills into the cavity of the mouth of the fasting person during vomiting, he must spit it out. However, if he swallows it involuntarily, his fast is still valid.

Uttering falsehood against God ﷻ, the Prophets, and the Infallibles عليهم السلام:

Issue 857: Uttering falsehood about God ﷻ, the prophets, and the infallibles عليهم السلام invalidates his fast, even if he repents later and admits to his lie.

Issue 858: There is no problem in narrating traditions found in books that one does not know to be lies, although it is recommended precaution to attribute them to those books.

Issue 859: If he reports words attributed to God ﷻ, the prophet, or the infallibles (عليهم السلام), believing them to be true, and then it becomes clear that they are lies, his fast is not invalidated.

Issue 860: If the fasting person knows that uttering falsehood about God ﷻ and the Noble Prophet ﷺ invalidates the fast, and he attributes something to them that he knows to be false, but later it is proven to be true, it is an obligatory precaution for him to complete his fast and make up for it later as well.

Issue 861: If the fasting person is asked, "Did the Prophet ﷺ say these words?" and he intentionally answers contrary to the truth, then based on obligatory precaution, his fast is invalidated.

Inhaling thick dust directly into the throat:

Issue 862: Based on obligatory precaution, the fasting person must avoid swallowing thick dust, such as dust raised from sweeping earthy ground, cigarette smoke and other forms of smoke. If he does so, it is an obligatory precaution for his fast to be invalidated.

Issue 863: There is no problem using an inhaler containing medicine to treat shortness of breath, and it does not necessitate the invalidation of the fast.

Issue 864: If dust and smoke enter the mouth and nose without reaching the throat, it does not invalidate the fast.

Issue 865: If a strong wind stirs up thick dust and the fasting person does not avoid it despite being aware of his fasting, and the dust reaches his throat, then based on obligatory precaution, his fast is invalidated.

Issue 866: If he forgets that he is fasting and dust or similar substances enter his throat, his fast is not invalidated. Likewise, if dust enters the throat involuntarily, his fast remains valid.

Submerging the entire head underwater:

Issue 867: If the fasting person intentionally submerges his entire head in water, then it is an obligatory precaution for his fast to be invalidated, and he must make up for the fast of that day.

Issue 868: There is no difference in the ruling of the previous issue, whether the body is submerged in water while dipping the head or only the head is dipped in water alone.

Issue 869: If he dips half of his head in water and removes it, then dips the other half in water, his fast is not invalidated.

Issue 870: If he deliberately submerges his entire head in water but some of his hair remains outside, it is an obligatory precaution for his fast to be invalidated.

Issue 871: His fast remains valid if he doubts whether his entire head entered the water.

Issue 872: If the fasting person falls into the water involuntarily and the water completely submerges his head, or if his head is forcibly submerged in water, his fast is not invalidated, but he must immediately try to take his head out of the water. Similarly, if he forgets that he is fasting and dips his head in water, his fast is not invalidated, but he must promptly try to take his head out of the water when he remembers.

Issue 873: Pouring water over the head or standing under a shower does not invalidate the fast.

Some Rulings on the Invalidators of Fasting

Issue 874: Fasting is invalidated by committing the aforementioned acts (eating and drinking... etc.) if done intentionally and by choice. However, suppose it was not intentional, such as slipping and falling into the water, eating by mistake, or something being forcibly put into his throat. In that case, his fast is not invalidated.

Issue 875: If the fasting person inadvertently commits one of the actions that invalidate fasting, then deliberately repeats it, believing that his fast has already been broken, his fast is invalidated.

Issue 876: If the fasting person is compelled to commit one of the actions that invalidate fasting, such as being told, "If you do not eat, harm will come to you or your wealth," he eats to avert harm, and then his fast is invalidated.

Issue 877: If the fasting person is unsure whether he has done something that invalidates fasting, such as whether he swallowed something of the water that was forced into his mouth, then his fast is valid.

Things That Are Detestable [Makrūh] for the Fasting Person

Issue 878: There are various detestable actions for the fasting person, including the following:

1. Engaging in any activity that weakens the body (such as bathing and giving blood).

2. Smelling aromatic plants (perfuming oneself is not detestable).

3. Wetting the garment that is covering the body.

4. Brushing teeth with a moistened wooden tooth stick (miswāk).

5. Having teeth extracted or doing anything that causes blood to come out of the mouth.

6. Tasting food or similar actions.

7. Pouring medicine into the nose if it does not reach the throat.

8. Pouring medicine into the eye, and putting kohl (eyeliner) if its taste or smell reaches the throat.

9. A woman sitting in water.

10. Touching and caressing one's spouse or engaging in any action that arouses sexual desire.

11. Excessive rinsing of the mouth.

Times When It Is Obligatory to Both Make up [Qaḍā'] a Fast and Give Recompense [Kaffārah]

Issue 879: Intentionally and by choice consuming things that invalidate the fast during the day in the month of Ramaḍān,[52] without a valid excuse according to Islāmic law, not only invalidates the fast but also necessitates making up for the missed fast day. Moreover, it also necessitates expiation [kaffārah; give recompense] for the

---

[52] Its rulings have been explained previously except for a person's sleep in a state of janābah without ghusl.

intentional breaking of the fast, whether or not the person was aware of the obligation of expiation.

Issue 880: If someone breaks his fast by consuming one of the things that invalidate fasting due to ignorance of the Islāmic ruling, such as being unaware that taking medicine, like other ingestibles, invalidates the fast, then his fast is invalidated, and he must make up for the fast of that day without having to perform expiation.

Issue 881: If someone performs an action he knows is prohibited but is unaware that it invalidates the fast, he must make up for the fast of that day and perform expiation as a precautionary measure.

Issue 882: If something exits from the fasting person's stomach to his mouth, it is not permissible for him to swallow it. If he intentionally swallows it, he must make up for the fast of that day and perform expiation.

Issue 883: If a person vows to fast on a specific day and intentionally does not fast on that day or breaks the fast, then he must make up for the fast of that day and perform expiation.[53]

Issue 884: If someone breaks his fast during Ramaḍān based on information about the occurrence of sunset from

---

[53] Expiation for breaking a vow (Kaffārah al-Nathr): Feeding or clothing ten impoverished people. If one cannot do so, fasting for three consecutive days is required.

someone whose news cannot be trusted, and later it becomes clear that sunset had not occurred, then he is required to make up for the fast of that day and perform expiation.

Issue 885: If someone intentionally breaks his fast, the obligation of expiation is not lifted if he travels that day.

Issue 886: Engaging in sexual intercourse invalidates the fast for both parties involved and necessitates making up for the fast of that day as well as performing expiation.

Expiation for Intentional Breaking of the Fast

Issue 887: The expiation for intentional breaking of the fast during the blessed month of Ramaḍān, in the sacred Islāmic law, is one of the following three options:

1. Freeing a slave.

2. Fasting for two consecutive months.

3. Feeding sixty needy people.

Since there are no slaves to be freed in our present time, the accountable person must fulfill one of the remaining two options.

Issue 888: If someone intends to fast for two consecutive months as an expiation for breaking the fast in Ramaḍān, he must fast for a complete month and one day from the second month, ensuring continuity, and it is permissible for him to separate the days in the remaining period.

Issue 889: If someone is obliged to fast consecutively and breaks the fast for one day without a valid excuse or begins fasting during a period knowing that it will be interrupted by a day when fasting is prohibited, such as the day of ʿĪd al-Aḍḥa or a day when fasting is obligatory, such as a day he must fast due to a vow, then the days he fasted before that are not counted, and he must recommence fasting anew.

Issue 890: If someone intends to fast for two consecutive months but is unable to do so due to a valid excuse, such as illness or menstruation (in the case of a woman), he should continue based on what he managed to fulfill after the excuse has ceased, and he does not need to restart the fasting anew.

Issue 891: It is possible to fulfill the feeding of sixty needy people in two ways:

1. Satisfying them with ready-made food.

2. Delivering a measure (750 grams) of wheat, flour, bread, rice, or other food items to each.

Issue 892: The destitute is someone who does not possess a year's provisions for himself and his dependents and cannot acquire them.

Issue 893: If a person cannot fulfill any of the three options for the expiation of intentional fast-breaking, he must feed as many needy people as he can, and as a precaution, he must also seek forgiveness. Suppose he is unable to feed any needy people at all. In that case, seeking forgiveness alone is sufficient by saying "astaghfirullah" [I seek forgiveness from God] sincerely in his heart and tongue.

Issue 894: If one is duty is to seek forgiveness due to his inability to feed sixty needy people, if he is later able to fast or feed the needy, it is recommended that he do both.

Issue 895: The one who seeks to give recompense for an intentional break of fasting wishes to feed sixty needy people (in the details mentioned in previous issues); if he was able to reach sixty needy people, he could not give two or more shares of the provision to one person. Rather, every single one of the sixty people must receive one portion. Yes, he can give the portions of family members of a poor person so that he spends it on them. There is no difference between the poor person, young and old, and man and woman.

Issue 896: If the fasting person commits multiple acts that invalidate the fast in a single day, then only one expiation is required. However, if his fast is invalidated by sexual intercourse or masturbation, he should make an expiation for each instance of intercourse or masturbation.

Issue 897: If a person breaks his fast in Ramaḍān due to engaging in prohibited sexual intercourse or consuming prohibited food or drink, he can suffice with one of the three options for expiation. However, it is recommended that he combine all three options if possible (freeing a slave, fasting for two consecutive months, and feeding sixty needy people).

Issue 898: When expiation becomes obligatory for someone, he is not required to fulfill it immediately, but delaying it to the extent considered negligence in performing the obligation is not permissible.

Issue 899: No additional penalties are added if several years pass without fulfilling the obligatory expiation.

Issue 900: There is no obligation to prioritize between making up for fasts and fulfilling their expiation, so he can choose to do either first.

Times When It Is Obligatory to Both Make up [Qaḍāʾ] a Fast

Issue 901: If one does not intend to fast during the day in the month of Ramaḍān, or he fasts for show [ostentation], or intends not to fast but does not commit any act that breaks the fast, he must make up for the fasting of that day without expiation.

Issue 902: If one is in a state of janābah during the night in Ramaḍān and does not wake up from the second sleep before the Fajr call to prayer, according to what is mentioned in Issue 844, he only has to make up for the fast, but he must refrain from acts that break the fast until sunset.

Issue 903: If one forgets to perform the ritual bath [ghusl; major ablution] of janābah in Ramaḍān and fasts for several days while in a state of janābah, he must make up for the fasting of those days without expiation.

Issue 904: In the pre-dawn meal [suḥūr] of Ramaḍān, it is permissible to consume things that break the fast as long as he has not become certain that dawn has arrived.

Issue 905: In the pre-dawn meal [suḥūr] of Ramaḍān, if he consumes something that breaks the fast without checking whether dawn has arrived or not, and it later becomes clear that dawn had indeed arrived, he must make up for the fasting of that day. However, if he does so after checking and knowing that dawn has not arrived, and it later becomes clear that it has, he is not obliged to make up for the fast.

Issue 906: It is not permissible to break the fast on a day of Ramaḍān before being certain that the sun has set.

Issue 907: If he becomes certain of sunset on a day of Ramaḍān due to darkness or if he is informed about sunset by a reliable source, then he breaks his fast, and later, it becomes clear that the day was still ongoing (i.e., the sun had not yet set), he must make up for the fasting of that day.

Issue 908: If he presumes that night has fallen due to clouds and breaks his fast, and later, it becomes clear that the day is still ongoing (i.e., the sun has not yet set), he is not obliged to make up for the fasting of that day.

Issue 909: If breaking the fast becomes permissible or obligatory due to some reason, such as being forced to break it or throwing oneself into the water to save a drowning person, then in such cases, he must make up for the fasting of that day without expiation.

Issue 910: If the fasting person rinses his mouth during ablution (as it is a recommended practice to rinse a small amount of water in the mouth and gargle) while being sure not to swallow the water, but inadvertently, the water reaches his throat without his choice, if it is for the ablution of the obligatory prayer, then his fast is valid. However, suppose it is for purposes other than obligatory prayer or ablution, such as cooling off, and the water reaches the throat. In that case, it is an obligatory precaution for him to make up for that day's fasting.

Issue 911: It is not permissible to rinse the mouth if one knows that the water will reach his throat involuntarily or if he swallows it inadvertently.

Rulings of Making up for a Qaḍāʾ Fast

Issue 912: If one faints and remains in a state of comatose and unconsciousness for a day or more, which necessitates missing the obligatory fasting, then he is not obliged to make up for the fasting of those days.

Issue 913: If one misses fasting due to intoxication, such as if he did not intend to fast, then his fasting is invalid, and he must make up for the fasting of that day, even if he abstains from the invalidators of fasting throughout the day.

Issue 914: If he intends to fast, then becomes intoxicated, and remains intoxicated for the entire day or part of it, then it is an obligatory precaution to make up for the fasting of that day, especially in cases of severe intoxication that necessitate the loss of reason.

Issue 915: In the preceding two issues, there is no difference between drinking the intoxicant being prohibited for him or not prohibited due to illness or ignorance of the matter.[54]

Issue 916: The days a woman breaks her fast due to menstruation or postpartum bleeding must be made up after the month of Ramaḍān.

---

[54] That is, he does not know that the liquid he drinks is wine/alcohol.

Issue 917: If the accountable person does not fast in the month of Ramaḍān due to illness, menstruation, or postpartum bleeding and dies before the end of the blessed month, then someone does not need to make up those days —which he or she missed—on their behalf.

Issue 918: If a person did not fast for several days in the month of Ramaḍān due to an excuse, and he does not know the number of the days he did not fast if he does not know the beginning of the excuse, such as if he does not know whether he traveled on the twenty-fifth day of Ramaḍān, in which case he would be accountable for six days, or he traveled on the twenty-sixth day, in which case he would be accountable for five days, then it is permissible for him to make up for the lesser number. However, if he knows the beginning time of the excuse, such as if he knows that he traveled on the fifth day of Ramaḍān but does not know whether he returned on the night of the tenth of Ramaḍān, in which case he missed fasting for five days, or he returned on the night of the eleventh, in which case he missed fasting for six days, then in this case, it is obligatory precaution to make up for the greater number.

Issue 919: If a person has to make up for fasting in the month of Ramaḍān for several years, then it is valid that he makes up for whichever he wishes first. However, suppose time becomes limited for making up for what he missed from the fasting of the last Ramaḍān, such as if he has to make up for five days from the fasting of the last Ramaḍān, and there are only five days left until the next Ramaḍān. In that case, it is an obligatory precaution to make up for the fasting of the last Ramaḍān.

Issue 920: If one is occupied with making up for the fasting of the month of Ramaḍān, and if there is no constraint on time, then it is permissible for him to break his fast before noon. However, if time becomes constrained, meaning that there are only as many days left until the next Ramaḍān as the number of days to make up for, then it is an obligatory precaution for him not to break his fast before noon as well.

Issue 921: In making up for the fasting of Ramaḍān, if one intentionally breaks his fast after noon, he must perform expiation by feeding ten needy people. If he cannot do so, he must fast for three days.

مسألة (922) إذا كان عليه قضاء صوم شهر رمضان من عدّة سنواتٍ، ولم يعيّن بالنيّة قضاء أيّ سنةٍ منها، فيحسب من قضاء السنة الأولى.

Issue 922: If he has to make up for the fasting of Ramaḍān from several years ago and has not specified in his intention to make up for any particular year, then it will be counted from the make-up of the first year.

Issue 923: If a person breaks his fast due to an excuse (such as illness or travel), and the excuse ceases before the next Ramaḍān, he must make up for the missed fasts.

Issue 924: If someone does not fast in Ramaḍān due to illness, and his illness persists until the next Ramaḍān, then the obligation of making up for the missed fasts is lifted from him, and he must instead provide a measure of food for a needy person for each missed day.

Issue 925: If someone did not fast in Ramaḍān due to illness, and he recovers after Ramaḍān but immediately encounters another excuse, and he cannot make up for the missed fasts before the next Ramaḍān due to this new excuse, then he must make up for the fasting of those days in the subsequent years. Similarly, if he breaks his fast in Ramaḍān due to a non-illness excuse, then falls ill after Ramaḍān, and cannot make up for the missed fasts before the next Ramaḍān due to the illness, then he must make up for the fasting of those days in the subsequent years.

Issue 926: If someone breaks his fast in Ramaḍān due to travel and remains in the state of travel until the next Ramaḍān, then he is not exempt from making up for the missed fasting days of the previous Ramaḍān, and it is recommended precaution also to pay the expiation of delay.

Issue 927: If he is unable to fast during Ramaḍān and also unable to make up for it before the next Ramaḍān due to physical weakness, then the obligation of making up for the missed fasting days is not lifted from him; rather, he must make up for them when he becomes capable. Similarly, if someone does not fast for several years and repents and resolves to make up for them, he must make up for all the missed fasting days. He remains accountable for the missed fasting days if he cannot do so.

Expiation of Delay[55]

Issue 928: If someone did not fast in Ramaḍān due to an excuse, and the excuse is lifted after Ramaḍān, but he has still not made up for the missed days by the time the next Ramaḍān arrived, then it is obligatory upon him, in addition to making up for the missed fasting days, to also provide a measure of food for a needy person for each day.

Issue 929: If someone intentionally does not fast in Ramaḍān, and he has not made up for the missed days without excuse by the time the next Ramaḍān arrived, then it is obligatory upon him, in addition to making up for the missed days and performing the expiation for intentional breaking of the fast, to provide an expiation of delay (as mentioned in the previous issue) to a needy person as well.

Issue 930: The expiation of delay is a measure of food, equivalent to 750 grams of wheat, flour, bread, rice, or other food items, given to a needy person.

Issue 931: If someone delays making up for the fasting of Ramaḍān for several years, then it is obligatory upon him, in addition to making up for the missed days, to also perform expiation by providing a measure of food to the

[55] This means expiation that is obligatory because it delays making up for the fast of Ramaḍān until the next Ramaḍān arrives.

needy for each day. Nothing further is obligatory upon him for the delay in subsequent years.

Issue 932: Someone obligated to provide a measure of food for each fasting day can give the expiation for multiple days to a needy person.

Issue 933: Ignorance of the obligation to make up for missed fasting days before the arrival of the next Ramaḍān does not exempt one from performing the expiation of delay.

Rulings of Making up for the Fasting of the Father and Mother

Issue 934: If the father, and as an obligatory precaution, the mother as well, did not fast due to a non-travel excuse, and they did not make up for the missed fasting days despite being capable of doing so, then it becomes obligatory upon the eldest child, after their death, to make up for their missed fasting days on their behalf, whether by fasting himself or by hiring someone else to fast on their behalf. However, if the missed fasting was due to travel, then it is obligatory upon the eldest child to make up for it on behalf of both parents, even if they did not have the time and capability to make up for it.

Issue 935: Based on obligatory precaution, the eldest child must make up for any intentionally missed fasting on behalf of his father and mother.

Rulings of the Traveler's Fasting

Issue 936: Traveling during the month of Ramaḍān is permissible, even if it is to avoid fasting. However, it is preferable not to travel except for a good purpose or necessity.

Issue 937: Fasting is not valid for a traveler during the blessed month of Ramaḍān, and he does not need to intend to stay in one place for ten days to fast.

Issue 938: If the traveler's duty regarding prayer is to pray qaṣr, it is not permissible for him to fast while traveling. However, if his duty regarding prayer is to pray tamām (such as if he intends to stay in one place for ten days or his work is travel-based), he must fast.

Issue 939: If a fasting person travels after noon, he remains fasting. But his fasting becomes invalid if he travels before noon and intends to travel from the previous night. However, if he intended to travel during the day, it is an obligatory precaution for him to continue fasting and make up for it after Ramaḍān as well.

Issue 940: If a traveler who had intended to travel from the previous night travels before noon, it is not permissible to break his fast before reaching the outer limit (ḥadd al-tarakhkhuṣ). However, if he consumes what breaks his fast before that, then it is an obligatory precaution for him to perform the expiation of intentional breaking of the fast during Ramaḍān. However, if he was unaware of the ruling of the issue, the expiation is not obligatory upon him.

Issue 941: If a traveler reaches his hometown or the place where he intends to stay for ten days before noon and has not broken his fast, he must fast. But if he has consumed what breaks his fast, he makes up for it later. If he arrives after noon, fasting is not valid for him.

Issue 942: If a person vows to fast on a specific day, such as the first of Rajab, and he is traveling on that day, then he must fast, and he is not obliged to intend to stay in a place for ten days.

Issue 943: If a person vows to observe a recommended fast on a specific day but does not specify that he will fast on that day even if he is traveling, then it is not permissible for him to fast if he is traveling, and he must not intend to stay in one place for ten days. However, he must make up for it later.

Issue 944: The ruling of choice between qaṣr and tamām prayers in the four sacred places (Makkah, Madīnah, Kūfah Mosque, and the shrine of Imām al-Ḥusayn) does not apply to fasting. Therefore, a traveler in these places has the option to perform qaṣr or tamām prayers, but his fasting of the blessed month of Ramaḍān is not valid for him (as a traveler there).

Issue 945: It is not permissible to observe recommended fasting while traveling.

Issue 946: In Madīnah, it is permissible for a traveler to observe recommended fasting for three days out of necessity without intending to stay for ten days.

Issue 947: In sinful travel, tamām prayer is obligatory, and fasting is valid, whether it is obligatory, such as during Ramaḍān, or recommended.

Issue 948: In sinful travel, if one abandons the intention of sin before noon and continues his journey for a permissible purpose, and if the remaining distance of the journey covers the distance prescribed by Islāmic law, even if non-consecutive, then he should perform qaṣr prayers, and he must break his fast.

Issue 949: In sinful travel, if one abandons the intention of sin after noon, his fasting is valid. However, completing the fast and making it up later is preferable.

The Travel Who Fasts Contrary to His Duty

Issue 950: If a traveler is not permitted to fast intentionally contrary to his duty, his fasting is invalid. If this happens during the month of Ramaḍān, he must make up for the missed fasting days. However, if he fasts out of ignorance of the ruling,[56] his fasting is valid.

---

[56] Meaning he does not know that fasting while traveling is invalid.

Issue 951: In the scenario of the previous issue, if someone fasts due to ignorance of specific details of the ruling, such as not knowing that fasting is not allowed during travel but being unaware that if one intends to stay for ten days, then changes his mind before performing a four-unit prayer, the ruling no longer applies to him, and it is not permissible for him to fast.

Issue 952: If a traveler fasts out of ignorance of the matter, such as intending to travel to a place that is actually a prescribed distance away but fasting due to ignorance of the distance, then his fasting is invalid.

Issue 953: If someone forgets that he is a traveler or forgets that fasting while traveling is invalid and fasts during the journey, then his fasting is invalid.

Individuals for Whom Fasting is not Obligatory

Issue 954: If a pregnant woman fears harm to her fetus or herself, she is not obliged to fast. In the first scenario (harm to the fetus), she must provide a meal for a needy person for each missed day (as compensation [fidyah][57]), and she must also make up the missed fasts after Ramaḍān. In the second scenario (harm to herself), she must make up for the missed fasts, which is also an obligatory precaution to provide compensation. The payment of compensation for

[57] Food must be given to the needy to compensate for leaving an act of worship for a valid excuse.

the pregnant woman who is still less than eight months pregnant is based on obligatory precaution.

Issue 955: If a breastfeeding woman (whether she is the mother of the infant or not, and whether she is a hired wet nurse or a volunteer) fears harm to the infant due to a potential decrease in her milk supply or dehydration, she is not obliged to fast. She must provide compensation for each missed day and make up for the missed fasts afterward. If the harm is to herself, providing compensation is an obligatory precaution.

Issue 956: In the two previous issues, if she does not make up for the missed fasts before the next Ramaḍān due to negligence, she must also perform the expiation of delay in addition to making up the fasts. However, if she delays due to a valid excuse, then expiation of delay is not obligatory upon her. If the excuse is fear of harm to her infant, she must make up for the missed fasts when she can. If the excuse is fear of harm to herself, she is exempt from making up the fasts, and she must provide compensation for each missed day.

Issue 957: The expiation and compensation of a woman are her responsibility, not her husband's, even if her fasting is missed due to pregnancy or breastfeeding. Similarly, the expiation and compensation of a child are not obligatory on their father. However, it is permissible for the husband or the father to pay the expiation or compensation on behalf of his wife or child through delegation on their behalf.

Issue 958: Elderly men and women who find fasting difficult are not obliged to fast. Instead, they must provide a measure of food (such as wheat, barley, rice) as compensation for a needy person for each missed day. If they are incapable of fasting altogether, providing compensation is an obligatory precaution. In both scenarios, if they can fast after Ramaḍān, it is recommended precaution to make up for their missed fasting days.

Issue 959: A person suffering from excessive thirst to the extent that he cannot bear it or finds it extremely difficult is not obliged to fast. However, in the second scenario (difficulty), he must provide a measure of food for a needy person for each missed day, and it is an obligatory precaution to provide compensation in the first scenario (unbearable thirst). If he can fast after Ramaḍān, it is recommended precaution to make up for the missed days.

Issue 960: The amount of compensation is the same as the amount of expiation of delay, which is 750 grams of wheat, flour, bread, rice, or similar food items given to a needy person.

Ways of Confirming the First of the Month

Issue 961: The beginning of the month is established by five methods:

1. The sighting of the moon by the accountable [mukallaf] person himself.

2. The testimony of two just witnesses, if a large group does not reject the sighting, and if there is no doubt about the credibility of these witnesses.

3. Popularity that necessitates knowledge or assurance.

4. The passing of thirty days from the beginning of the previous month.

5. The ruling of the religious authority.

Issue 962: The sighting of the crescent moon in the afternoon confirms the arrival of the lunar month, and the night following the sighting of the crescent is considered the first night of the month.

Issue 963: There is no difference between sighting the crescent with the naked eye and using optical aids such as binoculars or telescopes. Just as the beginning of the month is confirmed in the case of sighting the crescent with the naked eye, the beginning of the month is also established if the sighting is done through binoculars, a telescope, or a spyglass. However, verifying the beginning of the month through the reflection of the crescent image on a computer screen, where the accuracy of the sighting cannot be confirmed, is questionable.

Issue 964: The apparent size (big or small) and elevation or lowering of the moon, or the increase or decrease in its width, is not legitimate evidence that the crescent is of the first or second night. However, if the accountable person gains knowledge from them, he must act according to his knowledge.

Issue 965: The beginning of the month cannot be established through calendars or scientific calculations by astronomers unless certainty is attained from their statement.

Issue 966: If the beginning of the month is established in a city, it suffices for the residents of other cities that share the same horizon. The unity of the horizon refers to places where the possibility of sighting the crescent and the impossibility thereof are equal.

Issue 967: Mere confirmation of the crescent by the religious authority is insufficient for others to follow unless there is assurance of the crescent's sighting.

Issue 968: If the ruler declares that tomorrow is the first of the month, and his ruling encompasses the entire country, then his ruling is considered valid for all cities.

Issue 969: If the accountable person gains certainty or assurance at the beginning of the month by announcing an oppressive or corrupt non-Islāmic state about the sighting of the crescent, it suffices.

Issue 970: If the crescent is not seen in a certain city, but the radio and television announce the arrival of the month, and if their report is grounds for certainty or assurance of the crescent's sighting, then it suffices, and there is no need for further investigation.

Issue 971: Fasting is not obligatory if the beginning of the month of Ramaḍān is not established. However, if it is later established that it was indeed the first of the month, then making up the fasting of that day becomes obligatory.

Issue 972: If the beginning of the month of Shawwāl is not established through moon sighting, even on the horizon of cities that are adjacent and share a horizon, or through the testimony of two just witnesses, or the ruling of the ruler, then fasting on that day becomes obligatory.

Issue 973: Fasting on the day that a person doubts whether it is the last day of Ramaḍān or the first day of Shawwāl becomes obligatory. However, if it is later established during the day that it is indeed the first day of Shawwāl, then one must break the fast even if it is close to sunset.

The Parts of Fasting

Issue 974: Fasting is divided into four categories: obligatory, prohibited, recommended, and detestable.

Issue 975: Obligatory fasting includes:

1. Fasting during the blessed month of Ramaḍān.
2. Making up missed fasts.
3. Fasting as expiation.
4. Fasting on the third day of iʿtikāf.
5. Fasting as a substitute for the sacrifice during the pilgrimage of enjoyment.[58]
6. Fasting that becomes obligatory due to a vow, covenant, or oath.[59]
7. Fasting that the eldest son must make up on behalf of his father and, based on obligatory precaution, his mother.

---

[58] If the pilgrim in Hajj cannot buy a sacrifice and he cannot take a loan, he must fast for ten days in place of that. He must pray for three days during the pilgrimage and seven in his hometown.

[59] In reality, what is obligatory is fulfilling a covenant, vow, and oath. It does not mean recommended or commendable [mustaḥabb] fasting turns into obligatory fasting.

Issue 976: Prohibited fasting includes:

1. Fasting on the day of ʿĪd al-Fiṭr.

2. Fasting on the day of ʿĪd al-Aḍḥā.

3. Fasting on a day where it is uncertain whether it is the last day of Shaʿbān or the first day of Ramaḍān with the intention of Ramaḍān.

4. The recommended fast of a wife if it warrants neglecting her husband's [conjugal] rights.

5. Fasting by someone for whom fasting is harmful.

6. Fasting by a traveler except in circumstances highlighted as exceptions.

Issue 977: Fasting is recommended on all days of the year (except those days that are prohibited or detestable). However, certain days have a confirmed recommendation for fasting, including:

1. The first and last Thursday of each month and the first Wednesday of the second ten days of each month.

2. The thirteenth, fourteenth, and fifteenth days of each month (the white days).

3. The months of Rajab and Shaʿbān (either in full or partially, even for only one day).

4. The birthday of the Noble Messenger ﷺ (17th of Rabīʿ al-Awwal).

5. The Day of the Ascension (27th of Rajab).

6. The Day of Ghadīr (the 18th of Dhū al-Ḥijjah).

7. The twenty-fifth of Dhū al-Qaʿdah.

Issue 978: Detestable fasting includes:

1. Recommended fasting of a guest without the permission or against the host's advice.

2. Fasting on the day of ʿArafah if it leads to weakness, preventing one from performing the rites of ʿArafah.

Conclusion: Etiquette of Fasting and Etiquette of the Blessed Month of Ramaḍān

Issue 979: Completing recommended fasting until its end is not obligatory, so one is allowed to break his fast at any time he wishes. Moreover, if a believer invites him to food, it is recommended in Islāmic law to accept his invitation and break the fast.

Issue 980: It is recommended for the fasting person to perform the Maghrib prayer before breaking his fast. However, if someone is waiting for him, or if his intense desire for food prevents him from his heart being present in the prayer, then it is better to break the fast, and if possible, he should ensure to perform the prayer within its prime time.

Issue 981: It is recommended that some individuals refrain from consuming what breaks the fast during the blessed month of Ramaḍān out of discipline and respect, even if they are not fasting:

1. A traveler who broke his fast while traveling and returned before noon to his hometown or where he intends to stay for ten days.

2. A traveler who arrives after noon in his hometown or a place where he intends to stay for ten days.

3. A sick person who broke his fast and recovered from the illness before noon.

4. A sick person who recovered from the illness after noon.

5. A woman who became pure from menstrual or postpartum bleeding during the day.

6. A non-Muslim who embraced Islām during the day in the month of Ramaḍān.

7. A child who reached puberty during the day in the month of Ramaḍān.

Iʿtikāf

The daily hustle and bustle of life and the preoccupation with material pursuits sometimes lead humans to become heedless of themselves and God. However, amidst all this, extremely valuable opportunities allow individuals to cultivate "vigilance" and engage in "self-accountability."

One of these opportunities is "iʿtikāf," wherein people dedicate themselves to worship, supplication, solitude, disconnecting from worldly attachments, and working on purifying the soul, refining oneself, and cleansing it.

Issue 982: Iʿtikāf is when a person stays in the mosque with the intention of worshiping God and servitude to Him without leaving it.

Issue 983: The basic ruling regarding iʿtikāf is that it is recommended, but it may become obligatory[60] at times due to a vow, pledge, oath, or contract.

Issue 984: Iʿtikāf is permissible at any time when fasting is permissible, with its most preferable times being during the month of Ramaḍān and the best of those times being the last ten days of Ramaḍān.

---

60 In reality, what is obligatory is fulfilling a covenant, vow, oath, and contract. It does not mean that recommended or commendable [mustaḥabb] iʿtikāf turns into obligatory iʿtikāf.

Conditions of Iʿtikāf

Issue 985: There are seven conditions for the validity of iʿtikāf:

1. Sanity.
2. Intention.
3. Fasting.
4. Presence in a single mosque.
5. It should not be less than three consecutive days.
6. Continuity of stay in the mosque.
7. Seeking permission for iʿtikāf.

Issue 986: Puberty is not a condition for the validity of iʿtikāf, so iʿtikāf by a mumayyiz child—i.e., a child who can discern between right and wrong—is also valid.

1. Sanity:

Issue 987: It is a condition for the person observing iʿtikāf to be sane. Therefore, it is not valid for someone insane, intoxicated, or similar to them to observe iʿtikāf.

2. Intention:

Issue 988: It is a requirement for iʿtikāf, like all other acts of worship, to be accompanied by intention and seeking closeness to God. This means that a person's stay in the mosque should be solely for seeking nearness to God ﷻ, without any trace of showing off or pretense.

Issue 989: Since iʿtikāf begins from the dawn of the first day, the intention must not be delayed beyond that moment. However, it is permissible to commence iʿtikāf at the start of the first night or during it, and the intention continues until sunset of the third day.

Issue 990: It is permissible for the person observing iʿtikāf to stipulate during the intention the possibility of retracting from his iʿtikāf if an urgent matter arises, and he may leave the mosque even on the third day.

3. Fasting:

Issue 991: It is not valid to observe iʿtikāf without fasting. However, fasting does not have to be solely for iʿtikāf; fasting for reasons other than iʿtikāf suffices as well (whether it is obligatory or recommended, and whether it is for the person observing iʿtikāf himself or on behalf of someone else).

Issue 992: Iʿtikāf is not valid for those for whom fasting is not valid, such as the sick and the traveler.

Issue 993: If a traveler intends to stay for ten days or vows to fast during the journey, it is permissible for him to observe iʿtikāf during the journey. However, if he does not intend to stay for ten days or does not vow to fast during the journey, his fasting during the journey is not valid, and therefore, his iʿtikāf is not valid either.

4. Presence in a single mosque:

Issue 994: Observing iʿtikāf in one of the four mosques/masjids (the Sacred Mosque, the Prophet's ﷺ Mosque, the Mosque of Kūfah, and the Mosque of Basra) is the most virtuous. However, it is permissible to observe iʿtikāf in any masjid-mosque. As for non-mosque masjids, where congregational prayers are held and a just imām, observing iʿtikāf to hope for the reward is also valid there.

5. It should not be less than three consecutive days:

Issue 995: It is obligatory in iʿtikāf that it lasts for no less than three consecutive days, and it is permissible to revoke it before the end of the second day. If someone observes Iʿtikāf for two days, observing it for the third day becomes obligatory. There is no problem if one extends it beyond the three days (even if it is just one extra day or one extra night), and there is no specific limit to this extension. However, after every two days, observing iʿtikāf on the third day becomes obligatory.

Issue 996: The three days of iʿtikāf are calculated from the dawn of the first day until the sunset of the third day. Thus, the second and third nights are included in the iʿtikāf, and leaving the mosque during them is not permissible. However, the first and fourth nights are not part of the iʿtikāf.

6. Continuity of stay in the mosque:

Issue 997: If someone intentionally and by choice leaves the mosque (in cases other than necessity), his iʿtikāf becomes invalid, even if he was unaware of the ruling.

Issue 998: If someone leaves the mosque inadvertently, under compulsion, or due to a necessary reason, whether obligatory or recommended, worldly or religious, his iʿtikāf does not become invalid.

Issue 999: If one is compelled to leave the mosque due to a necessity, he must avoid unnecessary delays, such as sitting or resting in the shade, and he should not remain outside the mosque longer than necessary.

Issue 1000: In cases of necessity, if one stays outside the mosque for so long that the purpose of the iʿtikāf is lost, then the iʿtikāf becomes invalid.

7. Seeking permission for iʿtikāf:

Issue 1001: If a child's iʿtikāf potentially harms his parents, he must seek their permission. Rather, it is recommended precaution to seek their permission even if it is not potentially harmful to them.

Issue 1002: If a woman's iʿtikāf conflicts with her husband's rights, it is an obligatory precaution for her to seek his permission.

Prohibitions of Iʿtikāf, Its Expiation, and Compensation

Issue 1003: The person observing iʿtikāf is prohibited from:

1. Inhaling fragrances and aromatic plants for pleasure.

2. Engaging in sexual intercourse. It is an obligatory precaution to refrain from touching and kissing the wife with desire, as she would be an addition to the sanctity of iʿtikāf, which would invalidate the iʿtikāf.

3. Masturbation, as an obligatory precaution.

4. Engaging in buying and selling. Abstaining from all types of trade, including leasing, is an obligatory precaution.

5. Engaging in disputes and arguments concerning religious or worldly matters (if done to defeat the opponent and show off knowledge and virtue). However, if the argument is to establish the truth and correct the opponent's mistake, then there is no issue with it.

Issue 1004: The prohibitions of iʿtikāf are not exclusive to the daytime; one must also avoid them at night.

Issue 1005: If the person observing iʿtikāf is compelled to buy and sell to eat and drink and cannot delegate others or fulfill his needs without buying and selling, there is no issue.

Issue 1006: If the iʿtikāf is invalidated, and it was a specific obligatory act, it must be made up for. If it was obligatory but not specific, it must be resumed.

Issue 1007: If the recommended iʿtikāf is invalidated after the second day, it must be made up for. However, if it is invalidated within the first or second day, there is no obligation to make up for it.

Issue 1008: Making up for the invalidated iʿtikāf or resuming it (which are mentioned in the previous two issues) is obligatory only if it was not stipulated at the beginning of the iʿtikāf the ability to withdraw from it in case of an impediment.

Issue 1009: The expiation for invalidating the iʿtikāf is like the expiation for intentional fasting-breaking in Ramaḍān, which includes freeing a slave,[61] fasting for two consecutive months, thirty-one days, or feed sixty needy people.

[61] This is not applicable at present.

www.ingramcontent.com/pod-product-compliance
Lightning Source LLC
Chambersburg PA
CBHW030406130626
46549CB00004B/1647